CONTENTS

INTRODUCTION

We encounter a number of words everyday. Some words are familiar to us, but others are not. We try to cram the new words in our brains, but are not successful at times. The reason for this is that even a human mind has its limitations! It is not possible for us to remember all the words that we find unfamiliar everyday.

To top it all, there are some words that are extremely confusing. We generally end up using the wrong word at the right place. Such usage can cause lot of problems, misunderstanding and embarrassment.

The beauty of the English language has solved this problem, as the language consists of some important roots that form the basis of vocabulary in English. If we learn to recognise these roots, we can easily learn the meaning of these words. Even if we are unable to learn the meaning of the word, we would be able to recognise these words whenever we see them.

This book is an attempt in this direction. This book will introduce you to some of the most confusing words, so that you may be able to use the right word at the right time. This book will also introduce you to some roots, which are most commonly used and lastly, this book will help you to build a good vocabulary by providing a list of words that you can use in your daily conversation.

Part 1

CONFUSING WORDS

Given below are some of the most confusing words of the English language. All the words in the sets given below have been explained individually. Some of these words can be easily recognised by any of us, whereas, we have never seen some of them before. Study these words carefully in order to avoid using them in an incorrect manner in the future.

A

accent, dialect
An **accent** is a variation of pronunciation from the standard language. A **dialect** also strays from standard pronunciation, but in addition uses a different vocabulary and grammar.

accept, except

To **accept** is to receive something or acknowledge something. To **except** means to exclude, omit, leave out or reject something.

accident, injury

An **accident** is an unforeseen event, which need not necessarily result in **injury**. **Injury** refers to physical harm or damage. 'It was a spectacular accident and it was amazing that nobody was injured'.

actually, virtually, really

Actually and **really** mean 'in fact', both these words are much used and abused. 'Did he actually say that?' is the right way to use this word. 'Well, actually, I wouldn't mind a drink' is abusing this word. **Virtually** means 'in effect', substantially, mostly, for all practical purposes, not quite.

adverse, averse

They look and sound similar, but are used in very different ways. **Adverse** means hostile and damaging: 'I have also worked under extremely adverse conditions'. **Averse** indicates disinclination and reluctance: 'She is averse to spending her hard earned money'.

affect, effect

These two words have a profusion of meanings that produce a rash of confusions! To **affect** is to influence or to cause something to happen: 'All this drinking can affect your health'. An effect is a result: 'One effect of all this burning is the depletion of natural resources'. Other meanings are close, but not the same: 'The burglar effected entry by the skylight'; 'This movie never fails to affect me'. Remember that:

affect - cause - usually a verb

effect - result - usually a noun

affecting, affection, affectation

A troublesome trio! An **affecting** (something like a play) is one that stirs the emotions. **Affection** refers to the act or state of fondness and attachment to someone or something. An **Affectation** is a pretence.

after, afterwards

'He ran after the bus' means to follow, to chase or to seek, but **after**, like **afterwards** (and **afterward** in American English) also means following in order or later in time. **Afters** refers to desserts and puddings.

aggravate, exasperate

Aggravate means to make a situation worse. It is commonly believed that this word refers to being or getting annoyed, but **aggravate** does not mean to get annoyed. In order to **exasperate** someone, one can try mocking, irritating or annoying them, which would then **aggravate** their foul mood.

agree with, agree to

One generally **agrees with** a person, but **agrees to** a proposal or a suggestion. 'I agreed with her on that issue, but could not agree to her suggestion of the restaurant'.

all right

Alright, the most commonly used and accepted format, is wrong. Though one uses **already, altogether** and **almost**, one cannot use **alright**. Even the most eminent authorities on English insist that **alright** does not exist. The correct spelling of this word is **all right**.

alter, altar

Alter refers to changing something and **altar** refers to a place used for sacrifices: The constructor said to the Pope, "I'm sorry, but altering the altar is not possible."

alternate, alternative

Alternate means one after the other, to substitute or take turns. An **alternative** is an option, generally used when only one other choice is available. The same applies to alternately and alternatively: 'I have decided to study alternately, that is, on alternate days, or alternatively I can study at the end of the year for two months continuously'.

Although, though

Both these words are usually interchangeable. **Though** means 'despite the fact'. **Although** means 'even though'. It is simply a matter of what looks and sounds right: 'Although I was tired, I went for the party'. 'I went for the party, though I was tired'.

amateur, novice

An **amateur** is the opposite of a professional. An **amateur** takes part in an activity only as a pastime. A **novice**, on the other hand, is just a beginner, while a **tyro**, a word no longer used, refers to an awkward, untrained novice.

Among, amongst, between

One uses **between** to connect two people, objects or ideas. **Among** is used to tell the relationship of several people, objects or ideas. **Amongst** means the same as **among**. 'The sweets were distributed among all the children of the class'. 'This should stay between the two of us'.

amoral, immoral

An **amoral** person is someone, who is without moral sense or principles, whereas an immoral person is someone, who is not in conformity with the accepted social behaviour.

analysis, synthesis

Analysis is to examine something or to investigate something, whereas **synthesis** is the exact opposite of analysis. Synthesis means to put things together, to merge together or to build something from various elements.

anxious, eager

Anxious implies a degree of fear or apprehension, while to be **eager** is to be impatient, keen or enthusiastic:

'She was anxious to get to her office' is wrong. What is probably meant is 'She was anxious (about reaching late) and eager to reach office'.

anybody, anyone

Both these words are singular and they are used interchangeably: 'If anybody/anyone is there, would he please open the door?' is correct. However, one must keep in mind that a lot of objections have been raised to the use of the word 'he'. Considering the gender bias in question over here, one should use 'they' or 'their'. 'Would they please open the door?' **Anyone** is split into two words, when single persons or objects are being referred to. 'Anyone can eat any one of these sandwiches'.

any more

There is no word as anymore. If one tries to say the word aloud, one will notice that it comes out as two words, with the stress on 'more'? So, **any more** are two words and not a single word.

apparent, evident, manifest

Apparent means seeming to appear whereas **evident** means conclusive or according to one's calculations. **Manifest** is the strongest term, which refers to something being clear to both sight, as well as understanding.

around, round, about

All these words are used interchangeably, depending on a person's taste and preference. **Around** refers to going around the city or a place. **About** also refers to the same thing as around, but about is also used to show nearness to something. 'I stay about two kilometres away from the railway station'.

assume, presume

One meaning of **assume** is definite. The other refers to undertaking something, as in, 'He arrogantly assumed the role of the boss'. The other meaning, which is to suppose or to take for granted, is generally confused with **presume,** which means to take for granted irrespective of the reasoning or proof.

assurance, insurance

Assurance is life insurance, which is in the form of a policy. It makes certain that one would get an eventual financial benefit, whereas **insurance** is a pledge of payment given in lieu of damage caused by fire, accident or some other form of mishap.

assure, ensure, insure

To **assure** somebody is to give them confidence or to promise them something. To **ensure** is to make certain and to **insure** is to cover or protect financially.

authentic, genuine

Authentic is applied to something that has been produced by someone. It is the opposite of counterfeit, whereas **genuine** has a wider range of meanings and is generally used to imply some innate or original quality: 'This purse has been made from genuine leather'. 'The expert agreed that the painting was an authentic Picasso'

average, ordinary

To say that someone wears **average** clothes does not mean anything. The person actually wears **ordinary** clothes. **Average** should only be used in its mathematical sense, even though the word has different meanings: If five individuals can study for 5, 7, 9, 11 and 14 hours a day, then their **average or mean hours** is the total 46 divided by 5, which is 9.2.

B

back, behind, backward, backwards

Back is a true all-purpose word that describes a position at the rear, away from one, reversed or returning and many other meanings. It can be used in a number of ways including as a prefix and a suffix also. 'quarterback, backbite, backslide, back-seat driver'. In British English, we do not use 'in back of'. This expression is used only in American English. In Britain, we use **behind. Backward** is used as an adjective. 'It was a backward village'. Backward can also be used as an adverb in the form of **backwards,** but even **backward** is perfectly acceptable: 'She stepped backward/backwards'.

baited, bated

Bated means to lessen or reduce, whereas **bait** refers to the food that is used as a lure to catch something. 'He asked the people to bate the noise, while he was setting up the goat as a bait for the lion'.

balcony, circle, dress circle, gallery, stalls

In most of the theatres around the world, the **stalls** are at floor level. The **circle** is at the next level, moving upwards. The **circle** is usually divided into **dress circle** and **upper circle**. The balcony is at the next level and the **gallery is** at the very top.

baring, barring, bearing

These words are derived from **bare, bar** and **bear**. **Baring** means to uncover, **barring** means to obstruct and **bearing** means to carry.

because, since, on account of, owing to, due to

These words are very tricky. **Because** refers to 'the reason', whereas **because of** refers to 'by reason of'. **On account of** is used in order to qualify a phrase. **Since** is used to show a time lapse. **Owing to, on account of** and **because of** are used as synonyms. **Due to** means caused by and it always links the result with the cause. English users should not substitute **because** for **due to**: 'He had to buy new books because his exams were approaching'. 'He had to return some of the books because of their missing pages'. 'He could not study from the books on account of the missing pages'. 'He had been returning the books since two days'. 'His failure in the examinations was due to his not having the books'.

begin, commence, initiate, start, in agugurate

Though these words are almost the same, they are used in different contexts. **Initiate** and **inaugurate** are mostly used to describe the origination of a specific venture, for instance, a construction project or the foundation of a building. **Commence** can be interchanged with **begin**, but **commence** is more formal. **Start** means a certain abruptness: 'Students, start your test!

believe, feel, think

One **believes** with faith, one **feels** with one's senses and emotions and one **thinks** with one's mind: 'I believed he would pass, but felt that something was wrong and now I think he had not studied hard enough'.

beneath, below, under, underneath

Beneath and **below** are the opposites of **above** and they mean 'lower than'. Both these words are used to describe a position, but without reference to any scale. On the other hand, **under** and **underneath** are the opposites of **over,** both suggesting a sense of position and proximity. The difference between the two sets of words is quite faint: 'The water in the river was flowing well below the danger mark'. 'She has always worked under somebody or the other'.

beside, besides

Beside means 'next to' or 'by the side of', whereas **besides** means 'apart from', 'in addition to' or 'moreover': 'She wanted me to stay beside her for the entire occasion'. 'Besides, I could not do that'.

biannual, biennial, bimonthly

Biannual refers to twice a year, whereas **biennial** refers to once every two years. **Bi-monthly** can be either twice a month or once every two months. One can be more specific in the use of such terms by the use of words or phrases, such as twice-monthly, six times yearly, once every two months, etc.

Bible, bible

When one refers to the Old or the New Testaments, one uses the capital B, but one should use the lower case b when referring to 'in the context of'. 'His book on grammar is regarded as the bible of English language'.

billion

The **US billion** is a thousand million and that the **British billion** is a million million. Unfortunately, everybody does not refer to this considerable difference. So now, in Britain, a situation has arisen, where much of the time a **billion** refers to a thousand million. To be more specific, one can say or write 1700 million and not 1.7 or 0.0017 billion.

blond, blonde

Blond is used when referring to males and **blonde** is used when referring to females.

born, borne, bourne

Born is to take birth, whereas **borne** is to bear. **Bourne** was used in the old English to refer to a stream. It is now used only in the names of places, such as Littlebourne, Bishopsbourne, etc: 'I took birth on October 1'. 'The responsibility of every child is borne by their parents'.

both, each

Both refers to two things, whereas **each** refers to every one of the two or more things: 'Both the tickets were torn'. 'Each of the three tickets was a sheer waste of money'.

bravery, bravado, bravura, courage, heroism

Bravery refers to the readiness to face danger or pain. **Bravado** refers to the ostentatious pretence of bravery. **Bravura** refers to a display of daring brilliance, especially in an artistic performance. **Courage** refers to the quality that is required to meet confrontation or danger with a firm resolve. **Heroism** refers to an act of selflessness that generally surpasses normal human behaviour.

breach, breech

To breach is to break or violate, whereas **breech** (remember that breeches are the garment that covers the posterior) is the rear part of anything: 'The authorities were very angry, as the contract was breached by their own people'. 'We got the breech birth'.

broach, brooch

To broach is to introduce a subject, whereas a **brooch** is a piece of jewellery, usually fixed to the clothing with a pin: 'The subject of marriage was broached by my parents yesterday in the party'.

burgeon, burgeoning

Burgeon is often used incorrectly. It is used to mean growing or swelling. The actual meaning of burgeon is something that is starting to grow, or sprouting.

burglary, robbery, stealing, theft

Stealing and **theft** are synonyms. Both these words mean to take away something that belongs to someone else, without asking them. **Burglary** refers to entering the premises of somebody else with the intent to steal something or commit a felony. **Robbery** refers to stealing that is accompanied by violence or the threat of it.

C

callous, callus

Callous means being careless, whereas **callus** means a patch of hard skin: 'His callous attitude towards the animals made me very sad'.

can, may, could, might

Can mainly refers to possibility, whereas **may** is used to show remote possibility. **May** refers to permission and even **can** is used for the same purpose, but **may** is considered more polite and is used when seeking permission from elders or superiors. The same rule applies to **could** and **might**, as they are the past tenses of **can** and **may** respectively. We no longer use the word, **mayn't**. Instead of this word, we are now using **can't**. 'I can win the race (now that I have practised enough)' 'I may win the race (if I run fast enough)'. 'Yes, you can take part in the race': 'Yes, you may take part in the race' 'Could/might I take part in the race?'

capitol, capital

The **capitol** refers to the legislative building, whereas the **capital** refers to the city, in which the legislature is located. The Capitol in Washington DC is always referred to with a capital C. 'I went to see the Capitol, which is in the capital city of Washington DC'.

casual, causal

Casual refers to accidental, unplanned, a chance happening and a relaxed manner, whereas **causal** is the relationship between an effect and its cause: 'The causal element in the failure of their plan was the casual attitude towards the plan'.

catholic, Catholic

With a small c, **catholic** means wide-ranging, comprehensive, almost universal whereas with a capital C, it is used as the shortened form for the Roman Catholic religion: 'He had catholic tastes in food'.

cavalry, calvary

Cavalry refers to all those soldiers that are mounted on horses, camels or are on wheels. **Calvary** is the mount where Christ was crucified It is located near Jerusalem.

celibate, chaste

If a person is **chaste**, it means to be pure, modest and sexually faithful whereas if a person is **celibate**, it means that he has abstained from marriage and sexual intercourse totally.

centre, middle

The **centre** of anything is mathematically exact and measurable whereas the **middle** of anything is used in a more general sense.

Christian name, first name, given name

Christian name refers to the first or the given names of Christians only.

chronic, acute

Both these words are opposite in meaning. **Acute** means sharp and quick, whereas **chronic** means long lasting and recurring: 'The acute pain made me fell as if I was suffering from a chronic illness'.

claim, allege, assert, maintain, said

Claim is used when a right is demanded or asserted. It is generally used as a synonym for **declare, assert, protest** and **allege, which is incorrect. To allege** is to assert something without proof. It is nowadays used to imply guilt. **Assert** means to declare something positively. It is stronger than **said.** The main meanings of **maintain** are **hold, preserve** and **sustain,** therefore **maintain** is used as a supportive word. 'He went to England to claim the crown'. 'It is difficult to maintain one's health in this cat race'.

climactic, climatic, climacteric

Climatic refer to the condition of the climate. **Climactic** refers to a climax or a high point whereas **climacteric** is used to refer to an important period in life. It is usually used for male or female menopause.

colony, protectorate, dependency

A colony is a territory that has been annexed by another power. The colonies of the present day world are referred to as **dependencies**, and they have their own legislatures. For example, Belize, Cayman Islands and the Falklands. A **protectorate** is a territory protected and defended by a stronger state.

commonly, customarily, frequently, generally, habitually, ordinarily, usually

Commonly, generally, ordinarily and **usually** are used as synonyms. They mean 'normally' or 'as expected'. **Customarily** means 'according to the established custom or practice'. **Frequently** means 'often', whereas **habitually** means 'something that happens on account of it being a habit'.

compare to, compare with

Compared to is used to express dissimilarities while comparing two or more things. It is used to make a point. **Compared with** is used in order to make a note of the differences between two similar things. 'Her mother often compared her to her cousin'. 'You can't really compare Picasso's work with that of Goya's'.

compose, comprise, constitute

Compose and **constitute** mean the same thing, that is to form or to make up. **Comprise,** on the other hand, means 'consists of'. **Comprise** is a formal word, but this word is no longer being used: 'The house comprises of seven rooms'. 'The spell was composed of some strange things'. 'She hardly dared list the things that constituted the spell'.

complement, compliment, supplement

A **complement** is something that helps another thing to get completed. A **compliment** is an expression used to praise, someone whereas a **supplement** refers to an addition to something that is already complete. All these words are also used as verbs. 'She complemented the cake with a swirl of extra icing and a cherry'. 'He complimented her on her beautiful dress'. 'The doctor supplemented her diet with a a lot of milk products'.

concede, accede

Accede refers to a willing agreement, whereas **concede** refers to agreeing, but reluctantly and with grudges: 'He acceded enthusiastically to the idea of a picnic'. 'He conceded to his child going for a summer camp'.

conscience, conscious, conscientious

Conscience refers to the sense of deciding what is right and what is wrong. **Conscious** means the state of being aware, physically and mentally, of oneself. To be **conscientious** is to behave according to a set code of principles.

consecutive, successive

Consecutive means following without an interval or break, whereas successive means following in order, but not necessarily without intervals.

consensus

Consensus itself means 'an agreement of opinion': One must avoid using 'consensus of opinion'.

conservative, Conservative

If the word is written with a small c, it means opposed to change, moderate, cautious and conventional, whereas if the word is written with a capital C, it refers to a member or supporter of a Conservative political party.

consultant, specialist

Patients use the services of a **specialist,** while a doctor uses the services of **consultant.** This categorisation is strictly in the medical parlance.

continual, continuous

Continual means something that is repeated at short intervals, whereas **continuous** means without a break.

convince, persuade

Convince refers to proving something to somebody with the help of arguments and with the help of facts, whereas **persuade** refers to winning over someone with the help of reason or emotions.

correspond to, correspond with

Correspond with someone, refers to exchanging letters with them, whereas **correspond to** refers to being in harmony with or to tally with. A **correspondent** is one, who writes letters and a **co-respondent** is someone, who is 'the other party' in divorce proceedings. 'Your version of the story corresponds to her version of the story'.

couple, pair

Couple refers to any two things that have been united or joined together, for example, a couple of drinks or a married couple. A **pair,** on the other hand, refers to two things that are of the same kind. A pair is also mutually dependent, for example, a **pair** of scissors or a **pair** of gloves.

curb, kerb

Curb means to control or to restrain. In Britain, **kerb** is the edge of the pavement or the drop between paved footpath and the gutter. In the US, however, the **curb** refers to the edge of the pavement.

currant, current

A **currant** is a small, dark and dried grape. **Current** refers to two things, first a flow (of electricity, water, air) and second existing in the present time: 'With such a hectic routine, it is difficult to keep up with current events'.

cyclone, hurricane, tornado, typhoon

A **hurricane** is a violent gale with winds exceeding 75 miles an hour. **A cyclone** is a hurricane, the winds of which blow spirally towards a region of low barometric pressure. **Tornados** and **typhoons** are hurricane winds that rotate, creating funnel or cylindrical shapes.

cynical, sceptical

A **cynic** is one, who believes that there is little good in anyone or anything, whereas a **sceptic** is a doubter, who has a problem in believing anything unless and until it has been proved amply.

D

dais, lectern, podium, rostrum

Rostrum is a raised platform whereas a **dais** is a rostrum, on which lot of people can sit or stand. A **podium** is a platform used for a single speaker and a **lectern** is the stand, which the speaker can use to keep his notes on.

debar, disbar

Debar refers to excluding or shutting out, whereas **disbar** refers to expulsion, usually from a Court of law.

deceitful, deceptive

Deceitful refers to being misleading or cheating deliberately. **Deceptive** is used as an adjective to describe the effect of a misleading circumstance: 'The man made use of all the deceptive methods he knew in order to mislead me'.

decent, descent, dissent

Decent refers to being good, respectable and morally upright. **Descent** is a movement downwards and **dissent** refers to a disagreement.

decimate

To **decimate** means to destroy one out of ten, but it is widely used to indicate great destruction and even total annihilation.

defuse, diffuse

Defuse refers to the removal of a device or some circumstance that is likely to cause an explosion or an explosive situation, whereas **diffuse** refers to spreading. 'The infectious disease diffused through the air and the situation that was taking the shape of an epidemic had to be defused somehow'.

dependant, dependent

Dependant is a noun and **dependent** is an adjective. A **dependant** is one, who is **dependent** upon some form of physical, moral or financial support: 'It was well known that the hypothesis was dependent on the availability of proof'. 'The young man was dependant on his wife'.

deprecate, depreciate

Deprecate refers to expressing disapproval, whereas **depreciate** refers to lowering in value: 'The value of these shares have depreciated by more than half'.

desire, want, need

Need expresses the strongest requirement and urgency. **Want** refers to a less urgent craving, whereas **desire** refers to a degree of wishful thinking: 'He desired a simpler life, wanted a wife to stay with and needed to pay the rent'.

desiccated

Desiccated refers to dried and not chopped up, as commonly believed.

device, devise

A **device** is like an implement that has been designed or made for a specific purpose, whereas to **devise** something is to invent or create something: 'The man who devised the telephone gave us the device to stay in touch with other people'.

diagnosis, prognosis

A **diagnosis** refers to an identification of or an opinion about a problem or disease, whereas a **prognosis** is a prediction about the outcome.

differ from, differ with

To **differ from** means 'in contrast to', whereas to **differ with** means to disagree with someone: 'My choice of clothes generally differs from her choice'.

different from, different to

The correct expression to use is different from. The use of **different than** and **different to,** though is not incorrect, but it is also not preferred.

dinghy, dingy

A **dinghy** refers to a small boat, whereas **dingy** refers to something being grimy, soiled, shabby and occasionally, gloomy.

disc, disk

Disc is used for describing flat surfaces and **disk** is used for the hardware that is used in computers, for example, floppy disk. The usage of both these spellings is still neither uniform nor distinct.

discreet, discrete

Discreet refers to being careful, circumspect or prudent, whereas **discrete** refers to being separate, unattached or distinct.

disinterested, uninterested

Disinterested refers to being impartial or to be uninvolved, whereas **uninterested** refers to lack of interest in something or to be bored: 'He attended the meeting as a disinterested party'. 'He was completely uninterested in what was going on in the class'.

disorient, disorientate

Both these words mean the same thing that is 'to be confused' or to 'lose one's bearings'.

doubtful, dubious

Doubtful refers to something that is not clear, whereas **dubious** refers to something that has either doubtful manners or a doubtful character: 'She did not want to get involved in such a doubtful project considering the fact about the arrangement, especially with so many dubious characters involved'.

dual, duel

Dual two or double, for example, a dual carriageway, dual brakes, whereas a **duel** refers to a contest or combat between two adversaries.

dwarf, midget, pygmy

Dwarf refers to a human, animal or plant, whose growth has stunted. A **midget** is a very small person, whereas **pygmy** refers to a person, who belongs to a tribe, whose members are smaller than the normal humans.

E

eatable, edible

Eatable and **edible** can be used as synonyms. **Eatable** refers to something that is tastier than **edible:** 'The mushroom, once thought to be poisonous, is edible, although bitter'.

effective, effectual, efficacious, efficient

Effective refers to the action that produces the intended or the desired effect, whereas **effectual** refers to being capable of producing the desired or intended effect. **Efficacious** refers to having the power to produce the intended or desired effect, whereas being **efficient** refers to being competent: 'He was an efficient worker, effective with his tools, with a style that was effectual in clearing up all the work and above all, he believed in purchasing only those tools that were efficacious'.

egoism, egotism

Egoism refers to a person's unwarranted preoccupation with his or her own self and obsessive self-interest. An **egotistical** person is one, who is preoccupied with his or her own self, but reveals it to all with the help of excessive boasting and a predominance of I in conversations.

either, any, neither

Either means 'one or other of the two choices available'. **Any** refers to more than two choices, which are available. **Either** and **neither** are both used as singular words. One must never forget that either. . or go together and neither ... nor go together: 'Either go with us or stay with her'. 'There were two pens on the table and I didn't like either of them'. 'There were four pens on the table and I didn't like any of them'. 'Neither you are seeing things nor I am'.

empathy, sympathy

Sympathy refers to a sharing of emotions and a feeling of fellowship with another. **Empathy** is an extension of sympathy. It means a very close identification with the thoughts and feelings of another: 'The authoress revealed that she had an unusual empathy with the protagonist of her book'.

enervate, energise

Enervate means to drain and to weaken, whereas **energise** means the exact opposite. Energise means to fill with energy: 'A succession of hot, humid days generally leaves people irritable and enervated'.

enquire, inquire, inquiry

The difference between these words is not watertight. **Enquire** is used, when we are questioning something or someone, whereas **inquire** and **inquiry** are used in reference to an investigation: 'The official enquired about the results of the departmental inquiry'.

envious, enviable, envy, jealousy, covet

Envy is a part of the seven deadly sins. It refers to a feeling of discontentment and ill will at the advantage of others. **Enviable** refers to being worthy of envy. **Envious** is an adjective and is used for a person who shows envy. **Covet** is a synonym of envy. This means to lust after the possession of someone or something. **Jealousy** is the expression of personal unease about a situation, often involving rivalry, the transfer of affection or love to another or a suspected infidelity and tends to surface irrational behaviour, resentment and spite: 'She has bought herself an enviable car'.

especially, specially, exceptionally

Especially refers to something in particular, **exceptionally** means 'not ordinary', whereas **specially** means of a special kind': 'That bird is a special friend of mine'. 'I love blue, especially light blue'.

everyone, every one, everybody

Everybody and **everyone** are used interchangeable depending upon one's taste and preference. Both of them are used as singular words. When we refer to on a singular basis, then we can separate every and one:

'There were ten females in the room and every one was very well dressed'. 'There were ten oranges in the basket and **everyone** of them was rotten'.

evidence, proof, testimony

Testimony refers to the statement of a witness. **Evidence** refers to the information presented to support an argument and **proof** is evidence that is convincing that it dispels any doubts.

except, unless

Except means 'apart from', whereas **unless** is used when a person has to keep forward a certain condition. 'I will work everyday except on Sundays, unless you disagree'.

expertise, skill

Expertise is a better word for **skill.** Expertise has now acquired a broader meaning that encompasses special skill and knowledge that is also accompanied with experience.

F

facility, faculty

By **facility** we generally mean the ability to do something with a lot of ease. **Faculty** or **faculties** is used to make a reference to our natural or inherent powers, such as intelligence, sight, hearing, smell, taste, intuition, etc: 'He had the charming facility to make people extremely comfortable'. 'The project that he has decided to undertake will challenge all his faculties to the hilt'.

faint, feint

Faint means weak, feeble, indistinct or to lose consciousness, whereas a **feint** is an artificial or pretended attack that is undertaken in order to mislead.

farther, further

In the present day world, both these words are used interchangeably. **Farther** should be used with reference to distance and **further** is used when speaking or writing figuratively. Further is also used to show, 'in addition to'. 'He thought that Washington DC was farther than New York, but refused to think further about it'.

few, little, less

Less is used with singular nouns and **few** is used with plural nouns. **Little** is also used to describe plural nouns: 'This product is less fattening, a little expensive and has fewer calories'. 'Although I have little spare time, I do have a few to spare now'.

flout, flaunt

Flout means 'to show contempt or deliberately defy something or someone', whereas **flaunt** means to show off boastfully.

forego, forgo

Forego means 'to go before or to precede', whereas **forgo** means to do without or to give up something.

formally, formerly

Both these words are pronounced in the same manner, but are spelt in a different manner. These words often cause a lot of confusion. **Formally** is an adjective and is used to describe something that is done in a formal, ceremonious or established manner whereas **formerly** means in the past or at earlier times.

fortuitous, fortunate

Fortuitous refers to something that happens by accident or by chance. **Fortunate** refers to something that has a happy result: 'Our meeting at the party was fortuitous and fortunately she remembered the necklace I had loaned her a week ago'.

G

genteel, gentle, Gentil

Gentle means tender and kindly and it is the opposite of rough, coarse and violent. A **Gentil** is a non-Jewish person. **Genteel** originally meant well-bred and refined, but now it is mostly used in a mildly sarcastic way for ordinary people, who try to imitate middle-class lifestyles.

god, God

The Greeks had **gods,** whereas the Christians have **God,** the Supreme Being, which is always written with a capital G.

gourmand, gourmet, epicure, glutton

A **glutton** is a person, who will eat anything and any amount of it. A **gourmand** is a person, who, while appreciating what he's eating, loves to eat. A **gourmet** and an **epicure,** appreciate the finer points of eating and drinking, but for an **epicure,** the joy of food is almost a religion.

guarantee, warranty

A **guarantee** is an agreement to repair or replace, whereas a **warranty** is a promise that what is being sold is the vendor's and is serviceable and fit for the use claimed. Now a days, both these words are used interchangeably.

guess, suppose, think

To **guess** refers to putting forward an opinion. To **suppose** is to assume something to be true and to **think** is to arrive at a point of view by way of meditation or remembrance.

H

hire, rent, lease, let

Rent and **hire** is the money, which one pays for the use of something. To **let** a flat means allowing temporary possession of the property on payment of an agreed **rent.** Modern marketing has introduced a large degree of interchangeability in these words. One can now hire, rent or lease a car, a hall or a house. One, who lets his property is the **lessor** and one, who pays the rent is the **lessee.**

hitherto, previously

Hitherto means 'upto this time or until now', whereas **previously** means 'until then or prior to'. 'Hitherto we have ignored his unreasonable behaviour'. 'Previously, I never studied so hard'.

hotel, inn, public house, pub, bar

A **Hotel** serves meals and accommodation. It may or may not serve alcohol. **Public houses** or **pubs** are licensed, as are **inns** and **taverns** to serve alcohol. They may or may not serve meals and accommodations. All these terms are more or less interchangeable. All these places have **bars,** from where intoxicating drinks are served, but a bar can also be an establishment, such as a **wine bar** or a **gay bar.**

I

idea, opinion

An **idea** is a 'concept or a creation', whereas an **opinion** is a view, judgement, assumption or belief.

if, whether

'Did you notice whether or not he was present at the function?' We do not use, 'Did you notice if he was present at the function'.

illegible, unreadable

Illegible is usually taken to mean writing that cannot be deciphered due to fading out or damage, whereas **unreadable** is most often used to describe that sort of a writing that is bad, tedious or boring.

illiterate, ignorant

An **illiterate** person is one who does not know how to read and write, whereas an **ignorant** person is a person, who has little knowledge.

illusion, allusion, delusion

An **illusion** is used to describe or refer to a deception of the mind or the eye. An **allusion** is a passing reference to something or a passing mention of something and a **delusion** is a false belief.

in, in to, into

In refers to a place and is used for something that is static. **Into** is used to express motion and direction and **in to** is used to express the purpose of doing something. 'She is in the classroom'. 'She went into the classroom' 'She walked towards the classroom and went in to attend the lecture'.

inapt, inept

Inapt means 'unsuitable or inappropriate', whereas **inept** means clumsy or ill-conceived.

incredible, incredulous

Incredible means unbelievable or beyond belief. It is generally used to show a surprise or wonderful. **Incredulous** refers to the inability to believe. This is also an adjective.

infectious, contagious

Contagious diseases are those that are transmitted by physical contact, whereas **infectious** diseases are spread by germs in the air or in fluids.

infinite, infinitesimal

Infinite means 'limitless', whereas **infinitesimal** is used to describe things that are so small that they can easily be ignored: 'It is an unexplainable mystery as to why did the scientists took such infinite pains to measure such an infinitesimal difference'.

inflammable, flammable

Inflammable is used to describe something that is extremely **flammable.** It is generally thought that the prefix 'in' means 'not' and therefore inflammable means 'not flammable'. **Flammable** is used to describe things that can easily catch fire.

ingenious, ingenuous

An **ingenious** person is clever and inventive, whereas an **ingenuous** person is someone, who is open, frank and candid.

invariably, always

Invariably refers to something that is fixed, unchanged and never varying, whereas **always** refers to something that does is not interrupted at all. The difference is very slight and therefore, at times both the words are used interchangeably.

irony, sarcasm, satire

Irony is saying something that is the opposite of what one means with the intention of mocking. For example, you're waiting for a bus, the rain is belting down and you are being splashed by passing cars and suddenly the next man in the queue says, "Lovely day, isn't it?" **Sarcasm** is a bitter, derisory form of **irony**. **Satire** is the witty demolition of stupidity, wickedness and folly: 'Well, thanks for letting everybody know about my humble background!'

J

Jew

A Jew is a person, who follows the Jewish faith.

judicial, judicious

Judicial refers exclusively to justice and the law courts, whereas **judicious** refers to a good judgment, which is also prudent and expedient.

K

kind of, sort of, type of

All these terms are interchangeable. One must take care that the words **kind**, **sort** and **type** are all singular words. 'This kind of dress' in the plural becomes 'These kinds of dress' and not '**These kinds of dresses**'.

kipper, herring, bloater

All these words are used to refer to a sea fish called a **Herring**. When the herring is split, salted and smoked, it is called a **kipper**, and when a herring is cured whole without being split open, it is called a **bloater**.

L

laid, lain, lay, lie

To **lay** is to put or set down something, whereas to **lie** is to recline. **Laid** is something put down, whereas **lain** is something or somebody, who is reclining. **Laid** and **lain** are the past tenses of **lay** and **lie** respectively. **Lay/laying/laid; lie/lying/lain:** 'Lay down the law and lie on the floor'. 'After the hen laid the eggs, it went to lie down and rest'. 'The book was lying on the floor, it had lain there for days'. One must not use **lay** as the past tense of **lie.** 'She simply lay there and watched TV'.

lama, llama.

A **lama** is a Tibetan or Mongolian monk, whereas **llama** is a beast of burden of South American origin.

libel, slander

A **libel** is something written, published or broadcasted defamation of a person, whereas **slander** is spoken defamation.

licence, license

A **licence** is a noun and is meant to refer to a piece of paper, which is the evidence of permission granted, whereas a license is a verb that is the act of authorising: 'He was granted a licence to sell medicines and became a licensed chemist'.

lightening, lightning

Lightening means 'to lighten the burden', whereas **lightning** is when two clouds of opposite charges clash with one another.

literal, literary, literate, literally, littoral

Literal refers to actual. It should not be used to mean figuratively. **Literate** means having the ability to read and write. **Literary** means relating to literature and **littoral** is a shoreline.

loan, lend, lent

Loan is used for a financial transaction. One can raise a loan from the market. On the other hand, one can **lend** someone something. **Lent** is the past tense of **lend**:

'He raised a loan of £5,000 from the bank'. 'She lent me her car last month'.

loose, lose

Loose is used to describe anything that is free, hanging or unfastened, whereas lose is used to describe loss: 'She always wore loose clothing' 'The most feared criminal is on the lose again'. 'Give him any important paper and he is sure to lose it'.

M

majority, more, most, minority

More means greater in quantity, number, extent or importance. **Most** means the same, but it refers to an estimate. **Majority** also means more, but it refers to only those things that can be counted. The opposite of **majority** is **minority.**

malevolent, malicious, malignant

Malevolent is the closest to evil intent. **Malicious** implies a premeditated desire to hurt and injure and **malignant** means capable of harming to the extent of threatening life itself.

mantel, mantle

Mantel is the shortened form of mantelpiece, whereas a **mantle** is a cloak or a covering.

masterful, masterly

Masterful means imperious, domineering or self-willed, whereas **masterly** means extreme skill: 'With a flurry of masterly strokes he set the machinery right'.

may be, maybe

May and **be** are two words. **Maybe** means 'perhaps or possibly'. 'It may be wrong'. 'I may be unwell tomorrow'. 'Maybe I'll be unwell tomorrow'.

meantime, meanwhile

Both these words are interchanged a lot and are used as both nouns and adverbs. 'In the meantime, I studied all I could'. 'Meanwhile I completed my studies'.

media, medium

Media refers to all the newspapers, magazines, television, radio stations, cable, telephone networks and all those, whose business is communications together. Media is the plural of **medium**. 'The media of this country is extremely restricted'. 'TV is the most powerful medium to generate public opinion'.

meretricious, meritorious

Meretricious means 'superficial and flashy but empty and valueless, whereas **meritorious** means excellent and praiseworthy.

millennium

Millennium refers to one thousand years.

minimum, minimal, minimise, minuscule

Minimum and **minimal** mean the smallest or the least possible. To **minimise** is to reduce to the smallest possible amount, degree, extent or size and **minuscule** means anything that is extremely small: 'The minimal amount of food served at the boy's hostel is not enough'. 'He was charged the minimum prevailing rate'.

moral, morale

Moral is used to refer to what is right or wrong in human character and conduct, whereas **morale** is a mental state of confidence and optimism: 'The moral standards of the officers had an extremely bad effect on the morale of the soldiers'.

mortgagee, mortgagor, mortgage

A mortgagee is a person, who borrows money on behalf of a property and a **mortgagor** is a person, who provides the money for a **mortgage**.

Moslem, Muslim

Moslem was used in the olden times to refer to a person, who followed the Islamic religion. **Muslim** is the new term for the same.

must

Must is used to show extreme necessity and urgency, but in Anglo Indian, **must** is used to describe frenzied state of an elephant on heat.

mutual, common

Common means something that is shared by two or more or all, whereas mutual refers to something that is experienced, shared, or felt by two people: 'The boys' reluctance to share the cake was mutual'. 'In the end, the various warring factions of the nation found a common ground'.

N

nadir, zenith

Nadir is the lowest point of anything, whereas the **zenith** is the highest point of something.

naturalist, naturist

A **naturalist** studies natural history, whereas a **naturist** loves to enjoy natural surroundings, but in the nude.

nauseated, nauseous

Nauseous is used as an adjective. **Nauseated** is a feeling of nausea: 'The nauseous sight made me fell nauseated'.

necessities, necessaries, essentials

These words are again interchangeable and are used that ways. The difference between them is very slight. In usage, they have all come to mean about the same, which is why we are prone to add prefixes like 'bare necessities' and 'absolute essentials'.

negligent, negligible

To be **negligent** is to be careless and indifferent, to neglect something and often to a dangerous degree whereas **negligible** refers to unimportant, trivial or insignificant.

neither, none, nor

Neither means not either of the two options available. Neither is also singular just as either. Just as **either** is followed by **or, neither** is followed by **nor. None** simply means 'not one'. The experts on English have not been able to decide whether it is singular or plural: 'Neither of his two dishes, which we ordered were good'. 'Neither the blue trousers nor, the red trousers, have been washed today'. 'Not one of my dresses is washed'. 'None of my friends are coming for the marriage'.

net, nett

Net is the correct spelling and **nett** is wrong.

nevertheless, none the less

Nevertheless means however, yet or notwithstanding, whereas **none the less** means 'not any the less'. In America, **none the less** is written as one word: 'I was very tired, nevertheless I felt that I should humour the child'. 'Although I was none the less eager to play with the child, my tiredness prevented me from doing so'.

nice

This word has acquired a very very broad meaning. It is now used to cover anything from mildly sweet to exceptionally beautiful. It is therefore recommended that one uses more specific terms to describe or convey what one wants to say.

noisome, noisy

Noisy refers to a lot of noise, whereas **noisome** refers to something that is objectionable and offensive.

notable, noted, notorious

A **notable** person is that, who is distinguished by some aspect of worthiness or character. A person is noted due to some outstanding skill or achievement. If one is notorious, it implies that a person is famous for the wrong reasons: 'He was a noted basketball player'.

nutritious, nutritional

Nutritious, implies nourishing and not nutritional. **Nutritional** refers to the process of nourishing the body: 'The nutritional needs of a body demands at least three nutritious meals a day'.

❑

objective, subjective

Objective opinion refers to an opinion that is not influenced by any prior beliefs, personal feelings or prejudices, whereas to be **subjective** is to be the opposite or to be over-influenced by personal considerations or relationships.

obligate, oblige

Obligate refers to a moral or legal duty, while **oblige** implies to render a favour or to accommodate. 'The woman had obliged me on several occasions and now I felt obligated to repay her loan'.

obnoxious, noxious

Obnoxious is usually used to describe personal behaviour. This kind of behaviour refers to an extremely aggressive and unpleasant behaviour, whereas **noxious** is something that is potentially injurious.

obsolete, obsolescent

If something is **obsolete**, it means that it is out of use or outdated, whereas if something is **obsolescent**, it means that it is in the process of becoming **obsolete**.

obviate, obliterate

Obviate means to remove or to make unnecessary, whereas **obliterate** means to remove or efface by destruction: 'The new restaurant will obviate the need for people to eat at unhygienic dhabas'.

odious, odorous, malodorous

Odious means unpleasant and detestable, whereas **odorous** applies only to smells and might also be pleasant. In order to describe a bad or a foul smell, we can use **malodorous**.

official, officious

Official means the holding of a position of authority whereas **officious** means self-important and unnecessarily intrusive or nosey. 'The official incharge had glaringly officious mannerisms'.

off, of

Off and **of** are not used together. For example, 'He told us to get off of the bus'. This sentence is wrong. The correct sentence would be, 'He told us to get off the bus'.

one, one's, oneself

One is an indefinite pronoun. At times, the use of one can lead to inelegancy and pompousness, as any sentence containing it must use **one's** and **oneself**: 'No matter how much one wants to help one's country, it is not easy for one to put oneself in danger knowingly". Even the experts of English prefer the easier option, which is, 'No matter how much you want to help your country, it is not easy for you to put yourself in danger knowingly'.

ongoing, continuing

Ongoing is used to refer to anything that is 'in process'. Better choices for the same word are **continuing**, developing, etc.

on to, onto

Onto has been recognised as a single word only recently. Both these words are interchangeable.

opportunity, chance, possibility

Chance refers to the force due to which things happen without a cause. **Opportunity** is used when a person recognises a favourable opening and **possibility** is the likelihood of something taking place or existing.

ophthalmologist, oculist, optometrist, optician, ocularist

Ophthalmologists and **oculists** are medical doctors, who specialise in diseases of the eye. An **optometrist** tests eyes and vision and prescribes medicines, while an **optician** fills out prescriptions and makes and sells spectacles and an **ocularist** makes artificial eyes.

oral, aural, verbal

Oral refers to the mouth, so everything that is spoken. **Aural** refers to the ear, so everything that is heard. **Verbal** refers to words, spoken or written. The danger with this word is that if not used properly, the meaning of this word can be vague. An **oral** examination may be in the form of speaking. A **verbal** agreement may or may not be in writing. If one wants to mention or point towards a verbal agreement, then one can use the words, 'written agreement'.

orient, orientate

These words are used interchangeably just as **disorient** and **disorientate.**

orthopaedic, paediatric

In the olden days, an **orthopaedist** was a medical specialist, who treated deformities in children. But nowadays, an **orthopaedist** treats the bone, joint and muscle problems of children and adults, whereas a **paediatrician** treats children only.

overly

Though this word is used very frequently, its use is not preferred at all. The experts of English prefer saying, 'She is not over-enthusiastic about chocolates', rather than saying, 'She is not **overly** fond of chocolates'.

P

palate, palette, pallet

Palate is the roof of the mouth. A **palette** is an artist's board on which colours are mixed, and a **pallet** has a lot of meanings, but the most commonly used is a sound, timber tray, on which bulky goods are stacked so that they can be lifted and transported easily.

parameter, perimeter

A **perimeter** is a boundary or limit, whereas a **parameter** is a mathematical term for a constant, with variable values, used to determine a problem. **Parameter** is often misunderstood and misused.

part from, part with

To **part from** someone means to leave, whereas to **part with** something is to give it away or give it up.

partial, partially, partly

Partial can mean either prejudiced or incomplete. This calls for a very clear understanding of the term and using it should be well understood. A 'partial account' of some event could mean either things. The same meaning applies to **partially** also. **Partly** is used to denote a part of a complete thing.

passed, past

To **pass** from somewhere is to cross someplace, whereas **past** refers to something that was in the past.

per, a

Per is used in the context, 'We have worked for ten hours per day for the last month'. This means the same as 'We have worked for ten hours a day'. It is to be noted that the use of **'per'** is considered to be more sophisticated than the use of **'a'**. One also must note that the use of **per** is restricted to commercial or legal contexts, for example, in 'per annum'.

perceptible, perceptive, percipient

Perceptible refers to being observable or to being recognised or measured, whereas **perceptive** means 'quick to see and understand'. **Percipient** is almost a synonym, except that in this case the perceiving has a hint of the unexplainable about it.

peremptory, perfunctory

Peremptory means final, decisive and that which precludes any questions or objections. **Perfunctory**

refers to being careless and half-hearted. 'After drilling in such a perfunctory manner, the squad was peremptorily ordered to the cookhouse'.

permanent, perennial

Perennial actually means **permanent**, unfailing, unceasing, long-lived and not, as many people believe, 'year after year'.

perpetrate, perpetuate

Perpetrate means to commit something, to carry something out, whereas **perpetuate** means to preserve by making eternal. 'He perpetrated such a wonderful plan that the event was perpetuated by an annual lunch in its honour'.

perquisite, prerequisite

A **perquisite** is also called a perk. It means a benefit or privilege that is often regarded as a right, whereas a **prerequisite** is a precondition. 'One of the boy's prerequisites for a settlement was that nobody would take away the car parking perquisite from them at the hostel'.

personal, personnel

Personal is an adjective that is used to refer to something that is one's own, whereas **personnel** is a noun that means the staff of a company or organisation.

perspicacity, perspicuity

Perspicacity means 'clearness of understanding', whereas **perspicuity** means 'clearness of statement'. As

Eric Partridge once said, "Perspicacity is needed to grasp the distinction and perspicuity to explain it."

Peruse, read

Peruse means to **read** and examine carefully and critically.

petition, partition

A **petition** is a request, a plea or a formal written application to some authority, whereas a **partition** is a dividing wall.

possible, plausible, feasible

Possible means that something can exist, happen, or be done. **Feasible** means that something is worthy of being done, and **plausible** is an argument or statement that appears to be reasonable or true. 'The plan was not plausible, as it was raining very hard and it was not feasible to go out'.

practicable, practical, impracticable, impractical

Practicable means feasible, capable of being done and putting into practice, whereas **practical** has a wider range of meanings that includes useful, usable, sensible, realistic and efficient. 'It was practicable to climb the gate, but a more practical plan was to ring the doorbell'. Their opposites, **impracticable and impractical,** mean 'unfeasible, impossible, unattainable' and 'useless, ineffective' respectively.

practically, virtually

Practically means in practice, effectively, whereas **virtually** means almost or very nearly. 'After the war, people were practically starving, and clean air and water were virtually non-existent'.

practice, practise

'The lawyer had **practised** medicine for nearly forty years, thirty of them form his **practice** in Copernicus Road'.

precede, proceed, supersede

To **precede** is to go before, or come before whereas to **proceed** is to continue or to go forward. On the other hand, **supersede** means to displace or replace someone or something. 'As they proceeded to the altar, the bridegroom **preceded** the bride'. 'Many people were sad that the New Testament had superseded the Old Testament'.

predicate, predict

Predicate is increasingly being used as a synonym for **predict.** But, one must bear in mind that both these words have different meanings. **Predict** means to foretell, whereas **predicate** means to imply, affirm or assert. In America, predicate always means based. 'The teacher predicated that the questions would be tough, but declined to predict any of the questions for the examination'. 'His views on economic policy are predicated on the need to increase employment'.

pre-empt, prevent

Pre-empting is obtaining something beforehand or in advance, whereas to **prevent** is to hinder or stop.

premier, premiere

Premier refers to the first or the foremost, and is often used as a title for the country's leading statesman, whereas **premiere** is used only for the first performances of plays and films. 'The premier of that country will be present at the premiere of the latest Shah Rukh Khan flick'.

prescribe, proscribe

Both these words have opposite meanings. **Prescribe** refers to recommending a course of action or lay down some rules, whereas **proscribe** refers to the act of banishing or forbidding. 'In India, smoking is proscribed at all public places'.

principal, principle

Principle refers to a fundamental truth, a belief, a doctrine, an agreed rule of action or conduct. **Principal** can be used as an adjective or as a noun. Used as an adjective, it means of chief importance and used as a noun, it means the leader, the head, or a sum of money, on which interest accrues. 'The school principal said his principal aim was to make sure that all the students, who passed out form his school had strong moral standards and principles'.

program, programme

In British English, we still use the word **programme,** but **program** has made considerable inroads in the computer industry even in Britain. In American English, the word **program** is used.

prone, prostrate, recumbent, supine

All these words refer to lying down, but all of them are used in different senses and contexts. To lie **prone** is to lie face downwards. **Prostrate** is the same position as **prone,** but it also suggests a state of exhaustion and helplessness. **Recumbent** is lying in any comfortable position, whereas **supine** is lying listlessly on the back and looking upwards.

proposal, proposition

Both these words mean 'something that has been suggested' and are, therefore, interchangeable. **Proposal** is a suggestion and **proposition** is a stronger suggestion, or an assertion, that might result in a discussion before any agreement is reached.

purposely, purposefully

Purposely means on purpose or intentionally whereas **purposefully** means the same, but with added determination and with some definite purpose in mind.

Q

quantitative, qualitative

Quantitative refers to quantity and size, of amounts and volume, whereas **qualitative** refers to quality, of characteristics, properties, attributes and singularities.

quantity, number

One must use **number** only when the total can be counted, and one must use **quantity** for things that cannot be counted. 'To make the soup, you use a large number of tomatoes and a large quantity of water'.

quantum, leap

Quantum refers to an advance of unprecedented magnitude with no apparent connection with anything that preceded it. This term is used rather loosely. **Leap** is used to denote sudden increase particularly in quantity, or the act of jumping.

quorum, quota

A quorum is the agreed number of people that are required to be present before a meeting can be held, whereas a **quota** is a proportion, a limit or an agreed number or amount.

R

rain, reign, rein

One says that it is **raining** when water falls from the sky in the shape of drops that are larger than 0.5 mm. To **reign** is to rule, and **a reign** is a period during which a particular ruler rules. To **rein** is also to check or control and a **rein** also refers to the strap that controls and guides a horse. 'The constant rain of hurdles did nothing to stop Ashoka, giving full rein to his efforts of spreading Buddhism throughout his entire reign'.

raise, raze, rise

To **raise** is to elevate, whereas to **raze** means to destroy completely and to the level of the Earth. As one can see that **raze** and **raise** are total opposites. **Raise** also implies to 'rear children'. The experts of English, however, **raise** sheep and bring up a family. They also **raise** their heads, but **rise** in the morning and **rise** from their chair or bed. In Britain, the authorities still give one a pay rise, as against the American authority, which gives one a pay **raise.**

rapt, wrapped

Rapt means engrossed and absorbed, whereas **wrapped** means enveloped, enfolded or blanketed.

react, respond

A **reaction** is a response to some stimulus or provocation. Seeing it from this angle, **react** is an extremely vague term. In order to be specific, one must use the term that is more precise. One can use terms like **respond** and **reply.** 'His immediate response was to reply in the affirmative'.

rebut, refute, repudiate, deny

All these words have various meanings and are used in a varied manner. To **rebut** is to contradict with the help of an argument. To **deny** is to state that the given allegation or statement is false. To **repudiate** is to disown, reject or refuse to admit a charge or claim and to **refute** is to prove that an accusation is false. The last, that is, **refute** is the strongest word of the lot.

receipt, recipe

A receipt is a written acknowledgement that something has been received, whereas a **recipe** is a list of ingredients and the directions that should be followed in order to prepare a dish. However, it is an interesting fact that in the past receipt meant the same as recipe.

recoup, recover

Recoup means to regain or replace a loss, generally financial, whereas **recover** is used in a broader sense. 'When he recovered from the shock, he tried to comfort his family'.

reduce, lessen

Reduce and lessen are often used on an interchangeable basis. **Reduce** is used with everything that has to be lowered in quantity or quality, whereas **lessen** is used where numbers are involved in the quantity. 'By reducing his use of pesticides, he also lessened the number of apples that the trees bore for him'.

regretful, regretfully, regrettable, regrettably

Regretful and **regretfully**, both mean to feel sorry or to show regret whereas **regrettable** and **regrettably** are used when sorrow or regret is caused. 'Regretfully, I am forced to cancel our appointment. The problems caused by the cancellation are regrettable, but I will give you another appointment for the next week'.

regulate, relegate

Regulate implies to adjust, control or restrict, whereas **relegate** means to consign to an inferior position. Any football fan would be aware of the meaning of relegate.

reiterate, repeat

Repeat implies the making or saying of something once again, whereas **reiterate** tends to be used to express the repetition of a word, statement, account or request, often in order to stress it. One can see that there is a very marginal difference between the two.

relatively, comparatively

Both these words are used only when there is something to be **relative** to or something to **compare** with. 'Although it appeared to be an urgent project, it occupied relatively/comparatively little of his effort'.

replica, copy, facsimile

A **replica** is a duplicate that is made by the original artist himself or herself, or made under his or her supervision. A **facsimile** is a copy that is exact in every respect and detail, and a **copy** is the most general term that is used and it can be a duplicate, that is, a Xerox or a state-of-the-art colour reproduction or anything in between.

replicate, repeat

Replicate is increasingly being used as a synonym for **repeat**. **Replicate** implies rather more than that. A **replication** is the repetition of a study or of a research with the use of the same data and methods. This replication is done in order to confirm the results.

respectably, respectfully, respectively

Respectably implies in a way that is honest, decent and deserving respect. **Respectfully** means with respect and **respectively** means in the order given. 'Jasmine, Aster and Sarah are aged twelve, ten and three respectively'.

restful, restive, restless

Restful implies peaceful, calm, inviting rest. **Restive** and **restless** are the opposite to **restful**. A **restless** person is one who cannot be still or quiet, whereas a **restive** person is one, who frets under any type of constraint. Restive is an adjective that is commonly and generally used with horses.

restaurant, restaurateur

A **restaurant** is a place that offers meals for a price. It can also serve alcohol if it has the license to do so, whereas a **restaurateur** is a person who owns or manages a restaurant.

revenge, avenge

Revenge is personal retaliation, whereas, in the act of **avenging** the punishment is given by a third party as a rough form of justice. 'I eventually got my revenge by having him rusticated'. 'They avenged my brother's murder'.

review, revue

Revue refers to a type of a musical show that has loosely connected skits and songs, whereas **review** refers to an examination or an inspection. 'The revue had open to packed houses, but the savage review shattered the cast'.

rheumatism, arthritis

Rheumatism is a term that covers a variety of painful diseases of the joints and muscles, whereas **arthritis** is a term that points towards local inflammation of a particular joint.

S

saccharin, saccharine

Saccharin is a sugar substitute, whereas **saccharine** implies excessively sweet.

sacred, sacrosanct

Sacred implies dedicated to religious use, holy or not to be profaned, whereas **sacrosanct** is a more intensive term and it implies incapable of being violated, pure and that which cannot be corrupted.

sadism, masochism

Sadism is the desire to inflict physical pain on others in order to derive pleasure from the other's discomfort. This term is generally used for sexual pleasure. On the other hand, **masochism** is the desire to be physically abused or humiliated by another, generally for sexual pleasure.

salary, wages, remuneration

A **salary** is generally fixed as an annual rate and divided into months or weeks. **Wages** are rates paid on a daily or weekly basis and **remuneration** is a payment for a service, but not necessarily on a regular basis.

same, similar

Same means the exact number of something, whereas **similar** means resembling something or someone. 'Harish ate six breads for breakfast and the same for lunch'. 'I have a similar dress'.

sanatorium, sanitarium

In Britain a **sanatorium** refers to a quiet resort somewhere in the hills that offers curative services, whereas **sanitarium** is the American version of **sanatorium**.

sensitive, sensual, sensuous, sensibility

Sensitive is an adjective and is used for a person who is highly susceptible to influences, highly responsive to stimulus or is easily offended. A close synonym is **sensibility**, but this has come to connote heightened feelings for what is socially right. **Sensual** pleasures can be derived from physical indulgences like eating, drinking and sex, whereas **sensuous** refers to arousal through all the senses, for example, by listening to music, by smelling a flower, by watching a sunset, by feeling silk, etc.

sewage, sewerage

Sewerage means the sewage system and **sewage** means that what passes through it.

shall, will

When a person decides to use **shall** and **will** in the correct way and according to the rules, the number and the expanse of rules that govern their usage would frighten them. Due to the complexity of these rules, the distinction between the two has almost vanished. Their contractions, for example, I'll, she'll, he'll, etc. have now been adopted and are used everyday and on an extremely regular basis. The use of **shall** has finished and is now only confined to the 'official' documents. 'People shall take their shoes off before entering the temple'.

should, would

As we know that shall is no longer used in common parlance, so is should. The use of **should** has almost vanished, with **would** replacing this word at a very rapid speed. Instead of saying, 'I should like to see your work', we use 'I would like to see your work'.

silicon, silicone

Silicon is the chemical element which is in the form of sand. It has been used widely in order to reform the parts of humans as they want, for example, as breast implants to increase the size of the breast. On the other hand, **silicone** is a synthetic silicon compound that is used in order to make lubricants, water repellents and a range of other products.

simile, metaphor

A **simile** uses a direct comparison, usually preceded by as, as if, or like, whereas a **metaphor** makes an analogy. 'He fought like a lion'. 'The party was like a rock concert'. These two are similes. 'You're an angel', 'She's a dark horse' are example of metaphor.

A mixed metaphor combines two metaphors that are generally described as incompatible metaphors. 'We've got a real ice block on our hands'. 'This decision is a very bitter pill to swallow'.

sleight, slight

Sleight means dexterity, for example, the 'sleight of the hand' of a magician, whereas **slight** means small, slim or insignificant.

so-called

The use of this term is very critical. This term is used to indicate that what follows is to be held upto question or is to be ridiculed. 'The so-called people lovers said they had collected a petition of at least twenty thousand names for the upcoming elections'.

solecism, solipsism

A **solecism** is the violation of conventional usage. This is more or less confined to a faulty syntax and incorrect pronunciation, whereas **solipsism** refers to the theory that states that only the self is real and knowledgeable.

source, cause

Source refers to the starting point of something, whereas **cause** refers to that thing that produces an effect. 'The source of his headache was that blow to his head'. Actually the blow to his head was the **cause,** the **source** would be the reason why there was the blow.

specialty, speciality

Both these words are interchangeable. **Specialty** is preferred in the US.

stationary, stationery

Stationary means fixed, not moving or standing still, whereas **stationery** refers to all the writing material. This includes paper, pen, pencil, etc.

straightened, straitened

To **straighten** something implies doing it by making or bending it straight, whereas **straitened** implies restricted. 'Youngsters are always straitened under exacting circumstances'.

strategy, tactics, stratagem

Strategy is the planning of an operation. **Tactics** refers to the act of putting the strategy into effect and a **stratagem** is a scheme that has been designed specifically to deceive.

subconscious, unconscious

Subconscious has two meanings, firstly of being only partly aware, and, secondly, it refers to the thoughts that occupy the hidden level of the mind and influence our actions, whereas to be **unconscious** is to be unaware or to lose consciousness. 'She was unconscious of the fact that a person had been stalking her for sometime'. 'He does not know what happened after the accident, as he was unconscious for three days'.

substitute, replace

Both these terms have a subtle, but interesting difference. **Substitute** implies to put in the place of, whereas **replace** implies to put back again in place. 'She carefully replaced the bracelet, but substituted a cheap imitation for the priceless necklace'.

surely, certainly, definitely

All these terms do not have much of a difference. **Certainly** and **definitely** are interchangeable. Even **surely** can be interchanged with the other two words. However, **surely** can also mean safely and securely. **Surely** is also used to emphasise on a question. 'He made his way slowly but surely up the corporate ladder'. 'Surely you're not going to do that?'

swingeing, swinging

Swingeing implies severe in degree. **Swingeing is** pronounced as 'swinjing'. On the other hand, **swinging** implies that which has to do with a swing. **Swinging** as a slang also refers to being ultra-fashionable. 'People generally forget that the Swinging Sixties also saw a swingeing decline in the morals of the people'.

T

tartan, plaid

Tartan is the typical or a characteristic patterned cloth that is used for certain Scottish garments, including the kilt, whereas the **plaid** is a shawl that is worn over the shoulder.

tasteful, tasty

Tasteful is something that embodies or employs aesthetic discrimination or good taste, whereas **tasty** means flavourful to the palate, although colloquially it has also come to mean sexually attractive. 'The whole hotel was tastefully decorated'.

testament, testimony

A **testament** means the will or the document by which a person disposes of his estate after death, whereas a **testimony** is an evidence, a proof or a confirmation which is often given under an oath.

their, there, they're

This set of words are generally confused and misused. **Their** is a possessive pronoun. **There** means in or at that place, and **they're** is a contraction of 'they are'. 'It is their land'. 'She left her bag there, now it has disappeared'.

till, until

Both these words are interchangeable. **Till** is the shorter form of until. Both these words mean, 'up to the time when'. Though both are used equally, **until** is more preferred. 'I will wait until you return'.

that, which, who

That and **which** are relative pronouns that are becoming more and more interchangeable, even though, the rules that govern their use are different. However, some of the rules should still be followed and made use of. **That** is used to refer to persons, animals and things. **Which** is used to refer to animals and things. **Who** and **whom** are used to refer to persons. **That** is also used to restrict or define the meaning or intention of the preceding word or phrase. **Which** is used to identify the information that has already been supplied in the sentence. **That** is used to refer to any person, while **who** is used to refer to a particular person. 'The house that Hema had bought last week has burnt down'. 'The house, which Hema had bought last week, has burnt down'. 'The plumber that fixed this leak ought to be fired at'. 'My plumber, who was supposed to fix the leak, ought to be fired at'.

titillate, titivate

Titillate means to tickle or to excite, whereas **titivate** means to dress up in order to look extremely smart.

ton, tonne

An English **ton** is 2,240 Ibs. A short or American **ton** is 2,000 Ibs. A metric **tonne** is 1,000 kilograms or about 2,200 Ibs.

tortuous, torturous

Tortuous implies twisting, winding, devious, whereas **torturous** means inflicting torture and pain on someone. 'Following the dark, tortuous passages of the cave became a torturous nightmare for all of us'.

toward, towards

Both these words can be used interchangeably. The meaning of both these words is in the direction of or in respect of. One can use it according to one's taste and preference. 'They moved toward/towards the train'. 'The storm broke towards early evening'.

try and, try to

Try to is the correct form to use in an expression. Although **try and** is very common and is used as colloquial English, it is altogether right. 'She always tries to look down upon me'.

turbid, turgid

Turbid means clouded, muddy or opaque, whereas **turgid** means swollen, bloated or inflated. A river in flood can be both turgid and turbid'.

U

unaware, unawares

Unaware means that one is not aware or ignorant of something, whereas if one is caught **unawares,** it means that something has happened without warning and one is surprised. While **unaware** is used as an adjective, **unawares** is used as an adverb.

unique

Unique is used to describe those things that are different than the usual, something that does not have an equal or something that is one of its kind. It is used as an adjective. 'The coral that I saw yesterday was so rare and so exceptional, that I think it may be unique'.

unprecedented

Unprecedented implies first, original, unparalleled or unheard-of. One must, however, be careful when using this word, as the free usage of this word can lead to some major misunderstanding.

upon, on

Upon and **on** are almost interchangeable. However, there are some exceptions that are to be kept in mind. 'She sat upon/on the bed'. The exceptions over here are sentences like, 'Once upon a time, ... ' 'As far as the eye could see, the ocean stretched mile upon mile'.

urban, urbane

Urban refers to the city, as in urban living, urban architecture, whereas **urbane** implies poised, sophisticated or cultured. 'Only two years of urban life have transformed this country boy into a witty and urbane gentleman'.

use, utilise, usage

Use is synonym of **utilise** and **usage** and should be used as such. **Utilise** implies a narrow meaning of making useful or turning to a profitable account and **usage** is the recognised practice of something. It is also applied where quantities are to be mentioned. 'The company utilised the old warehouse to store the extra raw material'.

V

valuable, invaluable, valued

Valuable means having great value or being worth a lot of money, whereas **invaluable** means priceless, precious beyond valuation. **Valued** means extremely respected and highly regarded. 'I'm having my house valued', which means to estimate the worth of something. 'Her friendship at this difficult time was invaluable to him." 'Of all the things he valued most, her friendship was paramount'.

veracity, truth

Truth is something that is true, or that is a fact, whereas **veracity** is the capacity for being truthful, accurate and honest. 'We can depend upon his admirable veracity for the truth to come out'.

viable, workable

The meaning of **viable** is the capability to maintain independent existence in life. It has, however, become an overworked and inaccurately used word. One should try to limit its use to mean capable of surviving and thriving independently, whereas **workable** means something or some plan that is practicable and can be made to work 'Suicide is a viable alternative to painful terminal illness'. 'The Channel Tunnel is expected to be operationally workable by the year 2010'.

vicars, parsons, rectors

The differences between **parsons, rectors and vicars** are largely historic. **Parsons** and **rectors** were the most fortunate because their parochial posts included church property, income and revenue from the parish. The **vicar** got none of this, nor did the **curate,** who was an assistant to the parish priest. Their respective residences are called the **parsonage, rectory** and **vicarage.** A curacy is a position, not a residence.

vicious, viscous

Vicious implies a propensity for vice, hatred, spite and desire to hurt, whereas **viscous** means thick and sticky and is usually applied to liquids.

W

whatever, whatsoever

Whatever means no matter what, whereas **whatsoever** is vaguely synonymous in the context of 'at all' 'Whatever the problems, I promise to finish the job' 'Have you no manners whatsoever?'

X

Xerox

Xerox is a trade name, not a generic name and should be capitalised.

Y

your, yours, you're

Your means belonging to you, whereas **yours** denotes the particular one belonging to you. It is never spelt with an apostrophe, while **you're** is often confused with **your,** but it is a contraction of **you are.** 'I love your house'. 'Is that jacket yours?' 'You're quite mad!'

yours sincerely, yours truly

Yours does not have an apostrophe. If it did, it would mean 'your is'. **Yours truly** and **yours faithfully** are customarily reserved for impersonal letters. **Yours sincerely** is usedwhen the addressee is named.

Part II

Roots

Given below are some of the most commonly used roots. Once these roots are recognised and understood, it becomes relatively easy to use the various words in this language. Study these roots carefully and try to understand them, rather than memorising them.

CLAIM/CLAM = DECLARE, TO CALL OUT OR TO CRY OUT

The following words can be formed from this particular root.

1. claim: meaning, to call one's own, to ask for or to maintain.

2. reclaim: meaning, to make an effort to regain or to demand the return of.

3. claimable: meaning, that which can be claimed.

4. acclaim: meaning, to give praise to, for to applaud.

5. declaim: meaning to make a formal speech.

6.   declamation: meaning, a *recitation or an oration.*

7.   disclaim: meaning, cast *off, deny or disown.*

8.   exclaim: meaning, to cry *out, as with pain.*

9.   claimant: meaning, one, who makes a claim.

BL/BIN/BIS = TWO, TWICE

The following words can be formed from this particular root.

1.   biceps: meaning, a large muscle fastened in two places.

2.   bicuspid: meaning, a double-pointed tooth.

3.   bicycle: meaning, two-wheeled vehicle for travel, driven by foot-power.

4.   biennial: meaning, something that occurs at two-year intervals, or lasts two years.

5.   bimonthly: meaning, something that occurs every two months, such as a bimonthly magazine.

6.   biweekly: meaning, something that occurs every two weeks.

7.   bifocal: meaning, having two lenses, such as bifocal glasses.

8.   bigamy: meaning, the act of marrying one person when already married to another.

9.   biparental: meaning, born *of two parents.*

10.   bivalve: meaning, an animal with a shell of two parts which opens and shuts, as in clams.

VINC/VICT = CONQUER

The following words can be formed from this particular root.

1.   victim: meaning, one who is conquered and sacrificed.

2.   victimise: meaning, to make a victim of or to use as a sacrifice.

3.   victimiser: meaning, one who makes a victim of another.

4.   victor: meaning, one, who wins or a conqueror.

5.   victory: meaning, the winning, the conquest or the triumph.

6.   victorious: meaning, full of victory or triumphant.

7.   victoriously: meaning, *triumphantly.*

8.   evict: meaning, to throw out, as inevict a tenant who does not pay the rent.

9.   eviction: meaning, throwing out of house and home.

10.   convict: meaning, t*o prove guilty.*

INTER = BETWEEN, AMONG

The following words can be formed from this particular root.

1.   interaction: meaning, an a*ction for mutual advantage.*

2.   interaxillary: meaning, coming between two axils of leaves.

3.   interborough: meaning, *operating between boroughs.*

4.   intercede: meaning, to act between two parties in order to restore friendship.

5.   interdependent: meaning, mutually interdependent upon each other.

6.   interdict: meaning, to forbid as, to interdict trade with certain nations.

7.   intercept: meaning, to take between sending and delivery, such as intercept a letter.

8.   interciliary: meaning, *between the eyebrows.*

9.   intercostals: meaning, *between the ribs.*

10.   intercourse: meaning, correspondence or trade between or among people.

AN = NOT, ABSENCE OF

In this particular root, at times the n is omitted. For example, abyss, which means bottomless depth. 'An' should not be considered the same as 'not', or the same as the suffix 'an'. The suffix an means native of. The following words can be formed from this particular root.

1.   anecdote: meaning, a story or personal item not generally known.

2.   anecdotage: meaning, a collection of anecdotes.

3.   anecdotal: meaning, interesting or lively in conversation.

4.   anecdotist: meaning, one who tells anecdotes.

5.   anaemia: meaning, a condition in which there are not enough red blood cells.

6.   anaemic: meaning, deficient in red blood cells.

7.   anaesthesia: meaning, an absence of feeling or numbness.

8.   anaesthetic: meaning, an agent to produce anaesthesia, such as ether.

9.   anaesthetise: meaning, to *induce an anaesthesia.*

10.   anaesthetist: meaning, the physician who administers the anaesthetic.

11.   anodyne: meaning, creating an absence of pain or a narcotic.

MAN/MANU = BY HAND

The following words can be formed from this particular root.

1.   manual: meaning, related to the hand, as manual labour.

2.   manu caption: meaning, a document that was once used to obtain the presence in court of an alleged felon.

3.   manuduction: meaning, to lead by the hand or guidance.

4.   manacles: meaning, handcuffs or chains.

5.   manicure: meaning, the care of the hands and nails.

6.   manufacture: meaning, the act of making by machinery or hand.

7. manufacturer: meaning, one who hires others to make things in quantity by hand or by machine.

8. manufactory: meaning, a place, where merchandise is made.

9. manifest: meaning, seen at hand, obvious or apparent.

10. manumit: meaning, to release from contract, to set free, as in manumit a slave.

CRED = BELIEVE

The following words can be formed from this particular root.

1. credo: meaning, a set of opinions or a creed.

2. creed: meaning, a formula of faith or a set of principles.

3. credit: meaning, *value or worth.*

4. creditable: meaning, that which *can be believed.*

5. creditably: meaning, in such a manner that something is believed.

6. discreditable: meaning, n*ot worthy of belief.*

7. discreditably: meaning, n*ot believably.*

8. creditor: meaning, one who loans money to another.

9. credulity: meaning, a willingness to believe easily.

10. incredulity: meaning, a lack of willingness to believe easily.

11. credulous: meaning, inclined to believe readily.

ANTI/ANT = AGAINST

Anti must not be confused by ante. The following words can be formed from this particular root.

1. antacid: meaning, a remedy for acidity of the stomach or a counteracting agent.

2. antagonism: meaning, a strong feeling against a person or an idea.

3. antalkaline: meaning, an agent against alkalinity.

4. antapology: meaning, a *reply to an apology*.

5. antarchism: meaning, an antagonism to the government.

6. antarctic: meaning, the opposite of the north pole or the south pole.

7. antephialtic: meaning, the preventing of nightmares.

8. anthelmintic: meaning, expelling worms from the system.

9. antibiosis: meaning, antagonism between organisms in the body.

10. antibody: meaning, a substance in the body which opposes foreign substances.

UNI = ONE

This root comes from the Latin word meaning, 'one'. This particular root can be used to make a lot of words and that too with different meaning,s. The following words can be formed from this particular root.

1.   unicorn: meaning, a legendary creature with one horn.

2.   uniface: meaning, a design that appears only on one side.

3.   unify: meaning, to make into one.

4.   unification: meaning, the act of making into one.

5.   unifoliate: meaning, bearing one leaf.

6.   unilateral: meaning, one-sided.

7.   unique: meaning, one of a kind or having no equal, as in unique in excellence.

8.   unimanual: meaning, done with one hand.

9.   union: meaning, the joining of many into one, such as a trade union.

10. uniparous: meaning, producing one child or egg at a time.

11. unison: meaning, singing all the parts in one pitch as in the chorus sang in unison.

12. unitarianism: meaning, a belief in one God.

OPUS/OPER = WORK

The following words can be formed from this particular root.

1.   opera: meaning, a drama which has been set to music and is sung instead of spoken.

2.   operatic: meaning, resembling an opera or having qualities of the opera.

3.   operable: meaning, that which can be treated by an operation.

4.   operameter: meaning, an instrument for counting the rotations of a wheel in a machine.

5.   operalogue: meaning, a lecture on an opera which presents a summary of the story.

6.   operate: meaning, to labour, function or to perform surgery.

7.   operatee: meaning, the patient on whom an operation is being performed.

8.   operation: meaning, an action done as part of practical work.

9.   operational: meaning, relating to work performed.

URE = STATE OF, ACT, PROCESS, RANK

This root helps in making a noun out of an adjective. The following words can be formed from this particular root.

1.   censure: meaning, to find fault with or to blame.

2.   aperture: meaning, an opening or a hole, as an aperture in a wall.

3.   culture: meaning, the result of development in education, art and mode of life.

4.   exposure: meaning, the state of being laid open or bare of protection or concealment.

5.   immature: meaning, unripe or adolescent.

6.   future: meaning, that time which is yet to come.

7.   judicature: meaning, the court of justice or the judges collectively.

8. legislature: meaning, the collective body of persons who make the law.

9. overture: meaning, the opening piece of music in an opera, an introductory piece.

10. literature: meaning, the collective body of writings of the highest rank.

BIO = LIFE

The following words can be formed from this particular root.

1. biogenesis: meaning, the development of living organisms from life that already exists.

2. biogenesist: meaning, an expert in biogenesis.

3. biogenetic: meaning, pertaining to the development of life from life that exists.

4. biology: meaning, the study of living organisms.

5. biogeny: meaning, the development of life.

6. biogeography: meaning, that branch of biology that deals with the distribution of plants and animals.

7. biognosis: meaning, the investigation of life.

8. biography: meaning, the written story of the life of a particular person.

9. biographer: meaning, the one who writes about the life of another.

10. biographee: meaning, the person whose life is written about.

11. autobiography: meaning, one's own life story written by oneself.

PEL/PULS = DRIVE, PUSH OR THROW

This particular root is extremely violent. Not even one single peaceful word can be made from this particular root. This root is characterised by inner and outer turmoil. The following words can be formed from this particular root.

1. impulsion: meaning, an *uncontrollable impulse to act,* such as, an impulsion to *shoot,*

2. pulse: meaning, the beat or the heartbeat.

3. pulsation: meaning, the regular heartbeat or throbbing, such as, the pulsations of the wind.

4. compel: meaning, to urge or to force.

5. compulsion: meaning, the state of being forced or driven.

6. compulsive: meaning, *being forced, as* in compulsive *eating.*

7. compulsory: meaning, acting under compulsion such as compulsory education.

8. expel: meaning, to drive out or to throw out, as in expel from school.

9. repel: meaning, to *drive back, as in* repel *the enemy.*

10. propel: meaning, to push forward, as in the use of steam to propel ships.

SPOND/SPONS = PLEDGE OR ANSWER

The following words can be formed from this particular root.

1. sponsor: meaning, one who assumes the responsibility for a project, such as a sponsor of a charity.

2. sponsor: meaning, also to assume responsibility or to promise support.

3. sponsorship: meaning, the state of being a sponsor.

4. sponsorial: meaning, relating to a sponsor.

5. respond: meaning, to answer in kind, as in respond to a question.

6. response: meaning, an *answer, such as, an immediate* response.

7. responsive: meaning, causing to answer, as in a responsive nature.

8. respondent: meaning, one *who responds.*

9. responder: meaning, one who answers a communication.

CEDE/CEED/CESS/CEASE = GO, YIELD, SURRENDER

The various spellings used in this root are due to the use of a root that is Latin in origin. The following words can be formed from this particular root.

1.   cede: meaning, yield or admit, as in cede a point in an argument.

2.   accede: meaning, to go along with or to agree to.

3.   concede: meaning, *yield to or agree to.*

4.   secede: meaning, to do apart or to separate, as in secede from the Union.

5.   intercede: meaning, to go *between two litigants.*

6.   precede: meaning, to go before, as in the teacher should precede the rest.

7.   recede: meaning, to go back, as in the army begins to recede.

8.   precedent: meaning, that which went before, as in a precedent for a view.

9.   procedure: meaning, the manner of going forward.

10.   abscess: meaning, a localised collection of pus due to infection.

POLY = MANY

Innumerable words can be formed with the help of this root. The following words can be formed from this particular root.

1.   polyanthus: meaning, a type of plant, especially primrose, which has many flowers.

2.   polydactyl: meaning, having more than the normal number of fingers or toes.

3.   polychord: meaning, a viol-shaped instrument with ten strings.

4. polychotomous: meaning, that which has *many branches or many parts.*

5. polychotomy: meaning, division into many parts or branches.

6. polychresty: meaning, usefulness for many purposes.

7. polymorphic: meaning, having many forms.

8. polychromatic: meaning, *having many colours.*

9. polynomial: meaning, a *sum of two or more.*

10. polyclinic: meaning, a hospital where a variety of diseases are treated.

PER = THROUGH

The following words can be formed from this particular root.

1. per annum: meaning, in each year or for each year.

2. per capita: meaning, for each head or by each unit of population.

3. perforated: meaning, b*ored through, such as a* perforated *paper.*

4. perennial: meaning, through the years or eternal.

5. peradventure: meaning, a matter of chance or uncertainty.

6. peregrinate: meaning, to walk through or to travel, especially on foot.

7. perambulate: meaning, to walk through, to traverse or to promenade.

8. perceive: meaning, to understand or to take cognisance of.

9. perception: meaning, an act of knowing truths, insight or awareness.

10. perceptive: meaning, having a keen perception.

11. percolate: meaning, to drip through or to filter.

12. percent: meaning, the parts in the hundred.

13. percentage: meaning, the rate *of interest.*

MOB/MOT/ MOV = MOVE

The following words can be formed from this particular root.

1. mobile: meaning, *capable of moving.*

2. mobilise: meaning, *to assemble for movement, such as* mobilise resources.

3. mobilisation: meaning, the act of assembling for action.

4. mobility: meaning, the quality of being able to move.

5. motion: meaning, movement or action, such as make a motion.

6. motionless: meaning, *without motion.*

7. motive: meaning, cause, an inducement to move or a stimulus to act.

8. motivation: meaning, the reason for an action, the cause or the inducement.

9. mover: meaning, one *who moves.*

PRE = BEFORE

The following words can be formed from this particular root.

1. preamble: meaning, an *introduction,* such as *the* Preamble to *the Constituation.*

2. precaution: meaning, care that has been *taken beforehand.*

3. precede: meaning, to *go before.*

4. precedent: meaning, something similar that took place before.

5. predecessor: meaning, one who preceded another in office.

6. predict: meaning, to *foretell, such as* predict *the result.*

7. precipitate: meaning, to act hurriedly or to throw headlong.

8. preeminent: meaning, supreme or above all others, such as a preeminent speaker.

9. prelude: meaning, a musical or dramatic introduction.

10. premonition: meaning, a *forewarning or an omen.*

11. preoccupied: meaning, already occupied or very busy.

12. preparatory: meaning, *introductory,* such as *a* preparatory *school.*

DUG/DUCE/DUCT = LEAD

The following words can be formed from this particular root.

1.   abduct: meaning, to take away by force or to kidnap.

2.   deduct: meaning, to take away from, as in deduct ten percent of the price.

3.   deductible: meaning, that which can *be taken off such as tax* deductible.

4.   educate: meaning, to develop, to teach or to lead out from ignorance.

5.   induce: meaning, to lead into or to persuade.

6.   induction: meaning, the act of leading into an official position, as in induction into the army

7.   inductometer: meaning, an equipment used to measure electrical induction.

8.   introduction: meaning, the act of bringing in use or introducing.

9.   inductile: meaning, inflexible, unyielding or not easily led.

10. produce: meaning, to bring forth or to lead forward.

11. product: meaning, anything produced by growth, labour or thought.

12. productive: meaning, causing to bring forth or creative.

FLECT/FLEX/FLICK = BEND

The following words can be formed from this particular root.

1. flex: meaning, t*o bend, as in to* flex *the rod,*

2. flexible: meaning, a*ble to bend.*

3. flexibility: meaning, quality of being able to bend.

4. flexile: meaning, flexible or tractable, as in a flexile nature.

5. flections: meaning, t*he act of bending.*

6. flexor: meaning, a muscle which serves to bend a limb.

7. flexuous: meaning, relaxed, adaptable or not rigid.

8. flexuous: meaning, that which has *many bends or turns.*

9. genuflection: meaning, the *bending of the knee.*

10. deflect: meaning, to b*end away, as in* deflect *the missile from* its target.

11 inflection: meaning, the rise and fall of the voice such as the inflection of his voice.

12 reflect: meaning, turning back and forth in the mind, such as to reflect on a proposition.

METER = MEASURE

The following words can be formed from this particular root.

1.   mete: meaning, to measure or to assign by measure.

2.   meter: meaning, a measure or the official measure of certain commodities such as a gas meter.

3.   barometer: meaning, an instrument to record atmospheric pressure.

4.   meterage: meaning, the act of measuring.

5.   metrical: meaning, related to measuring or to metering.

6.   chronometer: meaning, an instrument which measures time.

7.   gravimeter: meaning, an instrument which measures weight and density.

8.   gyrometer: meaning, a rotary speed indicator.

9.   megameter: meaning, an instrument which measures longitude on the basis of the observation made after studying the stars.

10   macrometer: meaning, an instrument for measuring the size and the distance of objects.

PERI = AROUND

This particular root helps in forming words that are useful in all the subjects like in medicine, anatomy, geology, mathematics, dentistry, publications and, of course, space science. The following words can be formed from this particular root.

1.   pericarp: meaning, around the fruit or the covering skin.

2.   pericentric: meaning, deposited around the centre.

3.   periclitate: meaning, to expose to danger.

4.   pericranium: meaning, *around the skull.*

5.   pericardium: meaning, around the heart.

6.   periosteal: meaning, *situated around the bone.*

7.   perigee: meaning, that point in the orbit of a satellite that is the nearest to the Earth.

8.   perihelion: meaning, that point in the orbit of a comet or a planet that is nearest to the Sun.

9.   perigon: meaning, an angle that is round.

10. perimeter: meaning, the distance around a closed plane figure.

TRACT/TRAH = DRAW, PULL

The following words can be formed from this particular root.

1.   tractable: meaning, that which c*an be handled.*

2.   tractile: meaning, that which be *drawn out or tensile.*

3.   tractability: meaning, the quality which makes handling possible.

4.   intractable: meaning, that which c*annot he handled or is inflexible.*

5.   traction: meaning, the act of pulling or hauling.

6.　attract: meaning, to draw toward or to allure.

7.　attractive: meaning, alluring, such as, an attractive beauty.

8.　tractor: meaning, an automotive machine for farm work that pulls equipment.

9.　abstract: meaning, to draw away, as in to abstract money from the wallet.

10.　contract: meaning, an agreement that draws together, as both the parties signed the contract.

ASTER/ASTRO = STAR

The following words can be formed from this particular root.

1.　asterisk: meaning, a tiny star that is used in printing or to note something special.

2.　asteroid: meaning, like a star or resembling a star.

3.　asterozoa: meaning, form the starfish family.

4.　astrology: meaning, a study of the stars, especially the fact that they have an influence on the human destiny.

5.　astrologer : meaning, one who practices astrology.

6.　astrological: meaning, relating to astrology.

7.　astronomy: meaning, the science of the heavenly bodies.

8.　astronomer: meaning, one, who is versed in astronomy.

9. astronomical: meaning, relating to astronomy or enormous.

10. astrophil: meaning, one who is interested in star lore or an amateur astronomer.

11. astrophysics: meaning, astronomy and physics combined in order to understand the heavens.

12. astronaut: meaning, a *space traveller.*

IST = ONE, WHO, THAT, WHICH

The following words can be formed from this particular root.

1. accompanist: meaning, one who plays an accompaniment to a soloist.

2. alarmist: meaning, one who gets excited or alarmed needlessly.

3. artist: meaning, one who creates a work of art as a painter or a musician.

4. biologist: meaning, one who is versed in biology, the science of living things.

5. bigamist: meaning, one who is married to two wives at the same time.

6. chemist: meaning, one who is well versed in chemistry, the science of the composition of substances.

7. dentist: meaning, one who practises dentistry, the care of teeth.

8. evangelist: meaning, one who rouses religious fervour.

9.   violinist: meaning, one who is an artist with the violin.

10. humanist: meaning, one who is interested in human values.

POS/RON/POUND = PLACE, SET

The following words can be formed from this particular root.

1.   posit: meaning, set firmly in place, assert or declare.

2.   position: meaning, the manner in which a thing is placed.

3.   positive: meaning, *definitely laid down such as a* positive *law.*

4.   positor: meaning, one who asserts or affirms.

5.   post: meaning, a place, a station or a position, such as a soldier's post.

6.   postpone: meaning, place later or delay, such as postpone the wedding.

7.   posture: meaning, the placement of the limbs of the body or a carriage.

8.   posture: meaning, to assume a position or to pose.

9.   composition: meaning, a combination of parts to form a whole.

10. deponent: meaning, one who gives evidence in writing.

11. expose: meaning, set forth, show for all to see, as in expose a fraud.

POP = PEOPLE

This root is derived fro the Latin word populi, which means people. The following words can be formed from this particular root.

1. populace: meaning, *the people.*

2. vox populi: meaning, the voice of the people or the voice of God.

3. popular: meaning, related to the people, such as the popular vote.

4. popularity: meaning, the quality of being liked by many people.

5. popularism: meaning, a democratic movement.

6. popularist: meaning, one who believes in popularism.

7. popularise: meaning, to cater to popular taste.

8. populate: meaning, to furnish with people, as in populate a desert area.

9. population: meaning, the total number of people in an area.

10. populationist: meaning, one who advocates population control.

11. populous: meaning, full of inhabitants such as New York is a populous city.

LEG = LAW

The following words can be formed from this particular root.

1. legal: meaning, lawful or according to law, such as a legal holiday.

2. legalism: meaning, strict adherence to the law.

3. legalistic: meaning, strictly according to the law.

4. legality: meaning, the quality of being strictly legal.

5. legalise: meaning, to make lawful, as in to legalise abortion.

6. legacy: meaning, a gift of property left by will or an inheritance.

7. Legate: meaning, a delegate, an official messenger or an ambassador.

8. legate: meaning, to bequeath a legacy.

9. legatee: meaning, the one to whom a legacy is bequeathed.

10. legator: meaning, one who bequeaths the legacy.

11. legist: meaning, one who is skilled in law or a jurist.

12. legislate : meaning, to enact a law or to cause to become a law

HELIO = SUN

The following words can be formed from this particular root.

1. heliocentric: meaning, related to the centre of the sun.

2. heliochrome: meaning, a naturally coloured photograph.

3. heliochromoscope: meaning, an instrument that is used in order to produce photos in natural colours.

4. heliochromy: meaning, *colour photography.*

5. heliodon: meaning, a device to illustrate what seems to be the Sun's motion.

6. heliodor: meaning, a yellow beryl found in South Africa.

7. heliofugal: meaning, the tending away from the sun.

8. heliograph: meaning, an instrument for using the sun's rays.

9. heliogram: meaning, the message transmitted with the help of a heliograph.

10. helioid: meaning, like the sun.

TEST = TO BEAR WITNESS

This root should not be confused with the word test. The word test means an examination. Even in this word, we can see that one is the witness to one's knowledge. The following words can be formed from this particular root.

1. testate: meaning, leaving a valid will which has been signed and witnessed.

2.   testament: meaning, a will or an agreement of faith.

3.   testamur: meaning, a certificate attesting to proficiency, like a diploma.

4.   testate: meaning, to *make a will.*

5.   intestate: meaning, n*ot leaving a will, such as dying* intestate.

6.   testation: meaning, the act of making a will.

7.   testator: meaning, one who bequeaths his property by a will.

8.   testatrix: meaning, a *female testator.*

9.   testatory: meaning, of the nature of testimony.

10.   testimony: meaning, a *solemn declaration.*

MON/MONO = ONE

The following words can be formed from this particular root.

1.   monad: meaning, a *unit or one.*

2.   monandry: meaning, the custom of having only one husband at a time.

3.   monogyny: meaning, a society which establishes the law of one wife only.

4.   monarch: meaning, the ruler of an empire.

5.   monarchy: meaning, a government which has only one ruler.

6.   monastery: meaning, a religious institution, in which monks live.

7   monochord: meaning, an instrument that belongs to the olden days. This instrument had only one string.

8. monocle: meaning, an eyeglass for one eye.

9. monody: meaning, a funeral song or ode sung by one voice or a dirge.

10. monogamy: meaning, one marriage as opposed to bigamy or polygamy.

OID = LIKE, RESEMBLING

The following words can be formed from this particular root.

1. gynecoid: meaning, resembling a female in function.

2. asteroid: meaning, *like a star.*

3. dentoid: meaning, *like a tooth.*

4. helioid: meaning, *like the sun.*

5. hypnotoid: meaning, resembling hypnotism.

6. geoid: meaning, like the *figure of the Earth.*

7. geoidal: meaning, having the quality of the figure of the Earth.

8. anthropoid: meaning, *resembling a man.*

9. lipoid: meaning, *like fat.*

10. neuroid: meaning, *resembling a nerve.*

11. Negroid: meaning, resembling the Negro race in traits.

12. osteoid: meaning, *resembling a bone.*

13.   ostreoid: meaning, like an *oyster.*

14.   spheroid : meaning, *like a sphere.*

CREA = CREATE

This is the most important root in any language. The following words can be formed from this particular root.

1.   creant: meaning, to create or having the urge to create.

2.   create: meaning, to bring into existence or produce, such as create a song.

3.   creation: meaning, *the act of creating.*

4.   creational: meaning, relating to creation

5.   creationary: meaning, having the nature of creation.

6.   creative: meaning, having the power to produce such as creative ability.

7.   creator: meaning, one who creates or the maker.

8.   creature: meaning, anything that is created or a creation.

9.   re-create: meaning, to bring to existence again.

10.   recreation: meaning, the act of refreshing or renewal by food, exercise or rest.

11.   recreational: meaning, having the nature of refreshing.

12.   recreationist: meaning, one who is seeking recreation

THE/THEO = GOD

The following words can be formed from this particular root.

1. thearchy: meaning, the government under God.

2. theocracy: meaning, the government directed by priests or clergy representing God.

3. theocentric: meaning, that there is an assumption that God is in the centre.

4. theocrat: meaning, one who favours a theocracy.

5. theocratic: meaning, relating to a theocracy.

6. theocratically: meaning, in the manner of a theocracy.

7. theodicy: meaning, a defense of God's justice.

8. theody: meaning, a hymn in praise of God.

9. theogamy: meaning, the marriage of gods.

10. theolatry: meaning, the worship of God.

11. theologaster: meaning, a theological quack.

12. theology: meaning, the study of the elements of religion.

VERS/VERT = TURN

This root only tells one to turn. The direction in which to turn, is decided by the prefix that will be attached to the root. The following words can be formed from this particular root.

1. versatile: meaning, having aptitude for many skills, or one who is able to turn from one thing to another.

2. versatility: meaning, the quality of skill along many lines.

3. versation: meaning, a turning or a twisting.

4. versative: meaning, a*daptable or versatile.*

5. version: meaning, a changed form, an adaptation or a translation.

6. versus: meaning, against, as in a legal action of the state of Karnataka versus the state of Madhya Pradesh.

7. vortex: meaning, a double motion of whirling and pulling down or a whirlpool.

8. controversial: meaning, open to *disputes, like a* controversial *issue.*

9. averse: meaning, turned against such as averse to seeing him.

10. advertise: meaning, turn attention toward, such as advertise a book.

PED/POD = FOOT

The following words can be formed from this particular root.

1. pedagogue: meaning, one who leads a child or a teacher.

2. pedantry: meaning, a display of learning.

3. paediatrician: meaning, a doctor who specialises in the care of children.

4. paediatrics: meaning, that branch of medicine that is devoted to the care of children.

5. pedodontia: meaning, the treatment of the teeth of children.

6. pedophilia: meaning, inordinate love for children.

7. pedotrophy: meaning, the art of properly rearing children.

8. pedology: meaning, the study of *children*.

9. pedigerous: meaning, h*aving feet.*

10. pedestal: meaning, the base of a statue or a monument.

MICRO = SMALL, MINUTE

The following words can be formed from this particular root.

1. microaudiphone: meaning, an instrument to make slight sounds audible.

2. microlith: meaning, a *tiny stone implement.*

3. microbe: meaning, a minute organism or a germ.

4. microbicide: meaning, any agent which destroys microbes.

5. microcephalous: meaning, one that has *an abnormally small head.*

6. microcosm: meaning, a *small world.*

7. microcosmography: meaning, a description of man as a microcosm.

8.   microdont: meaning, one that has *small teeth.*

9.   microgram: meaning, one *millionth of a gram.*

10.   micrograph: meaning, an instrument for writing and engraving minutely.

11.   micrographer: meaning, one who specialises *in micrography.*

GEN = RACE, KIND OF

The following words can be formed from this particular root.

1.   genarch: meaning, the head of the family, tribe or race.

2.   gendarme: meaning, the cavalryman, who is in command of a squad.

3.   gender: meaning, kind, sort or sex, such as masculine, feminine or neuter.

4.   genitals: meaning, the reproductive organs.

5.   genealogy: meaning, the study of family lines or pedigree.

6.   genealogist: meaning, one *who traces genealogies.*

7.   gene: meaning, one of the elements that are responsible for hereditary development.

8.   genius: meaning, great natural endowment such as Milton was a genius.

9.   generable: meaning, that which *can he generated.*

10.   general: meaning, that which is *related to all kinds such as a* general *thing.*

PLU/PLUR/PLUS = MORE

The following words can be formed from this particular root.

1. plupatriotic: meaning, *showily patriotic.*
2. pluperfect: meaning, the past perfect tense.
3. plural: meaning, more *than one.*
4. pluralism: meaning, the state of one person holding two or more jobs at once.
5. pluralist: meaning, one who holds two or more jobs.
6. plurality: meaning, the state of being more numerous or majority.
7. pluralise: meaning, to make singular nouns plural.
8. plurative: meaning, more than half but less than all.
9. plurennial: meaning, a plant that lives for many years.
10. plurilingual: meaning, one who can *speak several languages.*
11. plurilateral: meaning, that which has *more than two sides.*

LESS = WITHOUT

The following words can be formed from this particular root.

1. baseless: meaning, without a base or groundless.
2. artless: meaning, without art or natural.

3.   careless: meaning, without care or slovenly.

4.   effortless: meaning, *without effort or easily.*

5.   friendless: meaning, without friends or alone.

6.   graceless: meaning, *without grace or clumsy.*

7.   fearless: meaning, without fear or unafraid.

8.   helpless: meaning, without help or defenceless.

9.   homeless: meaning, *without a home.*

10.   hopeless: meaning, without any expectations.

11.   listless: meaning, *without any spirit.*

12.   noiseless: meaning, without any noise or quiet.

13.   powerless: meaning, without any power or lacking strength.

LY = LIKE, MANNER OF

This particular root helps in making adverbs out of the various words. The following words can be formed from this particular root.

1.   carelessly: meaning, *in a careless manner.*

2.   baselessly: meaning, *groundlessly.*

3.   artlessly: meaning, *naturally.*

4.   effortlessly: meaning, *easily.*

5.   fearlessly: meaning, like one who is not afraid.

6.   gracelessly: meaning, *clumsily.*

7.   restlessly: meaning, like one who is unable to rest.

8.   hopelessly: meaning, like one who is without expectations.

9. listlessly: meaning, like one who is without any spirit.

10. noiselessly: meaning, without any sound.

11. powerlessly: meaning, like one who is without any strength.

12. helplessly: meaning, like one who is defenceless.

13. sleeplessly: meaning, *like one who cannot sleep.*

14. tirelessly: meaning, like one who never gets tired.

FUL = FULL OF

This particular root is very tricky in its usage. Generally the words are spelled incorrectly. One has to be very careful while using this particular root. The following words can be formed from this particular root.

1. frightful: meaning, able to make one full of terror.

2. careful: meaning, taking care or watchful.

3. doubtful: meaning, uncertain or having doubts.

4. grateful: meaning, full of thanks or glad to give thanks.

5. earful: meaning, full of news or gossip.

6. fearful: meaning, full of fear or frightened.

7. beautiful: meaning, *full of beauty.*

8. dutiful: meaning, fulfilling all duties.

9. helpful: meaning, willing to help or able to help.

10. graceful: meaning, full of grace or tactful.

11. hopeful: meaning, full of hope or expectant.

12. joyful: meaning, full of joy or very happy.

13.   mouthful: meaning, as much as the mouth would hold.

14.   pitiful: meaning, able to fill with pity or pathetic.

15.   restful: meaning, that which brings rest, like a restful sleep.

TRA /TRANS = ACROSS, THROUGH, OVER

The following words can be formed from this particular root.

1.   transatlantic: meaning, across or beyond the Atlantic Ocean.

2.   transcontinental: meaning, across the continent.

3.   transact: meaning, to put through a business deal.

4.   transaction: meaning, putting through of a business deal.

5.   transfer: meaning, to bring from one place to another.

6.   transferable: meaning, that which can be transferred.

7.   transmit: meaning, to send from person to person or place to place.

8.   transmitter: meaning, one who or that which sends across.

9.   translate: meaning, to change from one form to another, like to translate an article into another language.

10. translator: meaning, one who translates from one language to another.

PORT = CARRY

The following words can be formed from this particular root.

1. *port:* meaning, a place where ships may wait in or bring or take cargo to or fro from that place.

2. *porter: meaning,* one who carries things.

3. portable: meaning, that which can be carried.

4. *export: meaning, to* carry out. In other words, to bring or send elsewhere.

5. *exporter: meaning,* one who sells goods to other countries.

6. *exportation: meaning, t*he act of carrying goods out of the country.

7. *import: meaning, t*o bring in goods from a foreign country.

8. *importer: meaning, one* who brings in goods from a foreign country.

9. *importation: meaning, t*he act of bringing in goods from a foreign country.

10. *deport: meaning, to* send a person away or to banish.

IN/IM = NOT

If the root word, which follows the prefix, starts with a b, m or p, then the prefix will change from in to im.

The following words can be formed from this particular root.

1.   inability: meaning, the state of not being able.

2.   inadequate: meaning, not enough or insufficient.

3.   inaccessible: meaning, not reached to by people.

4.   inarticulate: meaning, not able to express oneself.

5.   inclement: meaning, not mild. It is often used for the weather.

6.   inhospitable: meaning, unwilling to be a host to others.

7.   intolerable: meaning, that which cannot be endured.

8.   insatiable: meaning, that which can never be satisfied or always wanting more.

9.   invisible: meaning, that which cannot be seen.

10. imperfect: meaning, that which has errors, or that which has flaws.

EN/EM = into, in

If the root word, which follows the prefix, starts with a b, m or p, then the prefix will change from en to em. The following words can be formed from this particular root.

1.   encamp: meaning, set up camp.

2.   encourage: meaning, to put one's heart into something, such as encourage with hope or spirit.

3.   endanger: meaning, to put into danger.

4.   enrol: meaning, to enter or to register.

5. enslave: meaning, to put into slavery or to make a slave of.

6. entrap: meaning, t*o catch in a trap.*

7. envenom: meaning, to poison.

8. environ: meaning, to put a ring around or to encircle.

9. environment: meaning, the life that surrounds one.

10. embark: meaning, to get onto a train or a ship for a journey.

11. embrace: meaning, to take into one's arms.

12. embitter: meaning, t*o make bitter.*

13. employ: meaning, t*o find a use for.*

14. embody: meaning, to give a body to something, such as a law must embody freedom.

IL/IR = NOT

The following words can be formed from this particular root.

1. illegal: meaning, n*ot according to law.*

2. illegible: meaning, not able to be read.

3. illiterate: meaning, having little education or that which cannot read or write.

4. illiteracy : meaning, the state of being uneducated or the inability to read or write.

5. illusion: meaning, an unreal image.

6. illogical: meaning, not having any sense or logic.

7. illiberal: meaning, not open minded or being a bigot.

8. illicit: meaning, not allowed or not lawful.

9. irreclaimable: meaning, that which *cannot be claimed again.*

10. irregular: meaning, *not as it should be.*

11. irreligious: meaning, *lacking religious feelings.*

12. irreverent: meaning, showing a lack of respect for holy matters.

13. irreparable: meaning, that which *cannot be repaired.*

FER = BRING, BEAR, YIELD

It is amongst the most commonly used keys. The following words can be formed from this particular root.

1. coniferous: meaning, bearing cones.

2. circumference: meaning, the line that goes around a circular plane.

3. deference: meaning, *respect for or courtesy.*

4. fertile: meaning, bearing good fruit or yielding much.

5. fertilisation: meaning, the act of causing to bear richly.

6. cross-fertilisation: meaning, fertilisation from one type to another.

7. conference: meaning, a bringing together or a meeting.

8. reference: meaning, a thought relating to a subject.

9. inference: meaning, carrying over a truth from one point to another.

10. odoriferous: meaning, bearing an odour, but usually pleasant.

11. preference: meaning, bringing forward.

12. suffer: meaning, to bear sorrow or pain.

EN = MADE OF, MAKE

En means made of, when it is used as an adjective and it means make, when it is used as a verb. The following words can be formed from this particular root.

1. silken: meaning, *made of silk.*

2. brazen: meaning, *made of brass.*

3. frozen: meaning, *made icy.*

4. hempen: meaning, made of hemp.

5. molten: meaning, made by melting.

6. oaken: meaning, *made of oak.*

7. woollen: meaning, *made of wool.*

8. wooden: meaning, *made of wood.*

9. golden: meaning, *made of gold.*

10. broaden: meaning, *make broad or widen.*

11. brighten: meaning, *make bright.*

12. hasten: meaning, make haste or put on speed.

13. heighten: meaning, *make high or increase.*

IN/IM = IN, INTO

In this particular root also, in becomes im, if it is used before b, m, or p. The following words can be formed from this particular root.

1. interior: meaning, the inside or the inner part.
2. influx: meaning, an inward flow.
3. ingress: meaning, the act of entering or coming in.
4. inhale: meaning, t*o breathe in.*
5. imbue: meaning, to inspire, such as to imbue with a love for chocolates.
6. imbibe: meaning, to drink in or to take into the mind, as in to imbibe culture.
7. immure: meaning, to wall in or to build a wall around.
8. immigrate: meaning, to come into a country in order to settle.
9. immigrant: meaning, one who comes into a country.
10. imminent: meaning, a*bout to occur.*
11. immingle: meaning, mix with, to join or to blend.
12. important: meaning, to h*ave a significance.*

FIC/FECT = MAKE

This is also one of the most used roots. The following words can be formed from this particular root.

1. beneficiary: meaning, one who receives a benefit.

2. deification: meaning, making a God out of something.

3. amplification: meaning, an *enlargement.*

4. acidification: meaning, an act or the process of making into acid.

5. calorific: meaning, that which produces *heat.*

6. certificate: meaning, a *written proof of a fact.*

7. confection: meaning, the act or process of making something,especially by combining or mixing.

8. affect: meaning, to m*ake an impression upon.*

9. defective: meaning, lacking *in something or faulty.*

10. deficiency: meaning, *something lacking.*

ARY/ERY/ORY = RELATING TO, QUALITY, THE PLACE WHERE

When used as an adjective, this root means relating to and when used as a verb, this root means a certain quality or shows the place where. The following words can be formed from this particular root.

1. burglary: meaning, the act of breaking into a place in order to steal.

2. dictionary: meaning, a book of words and their meaning,s.

3. dietary: meaning, r*elating to diet such as* dietary *laws.*

4. necessary: r*elating to need, like* necessary *food.*

5. primary: meaning, relating to first things or important things.

6. voluntary: meaning, r*elating to free will, such as, a* voluntary service.

7. bakery: meaning, a place where sweets, cakes and pastries are baked or sold.

8. bindery: meaning, a place where books are bound.

9. bravery: meaning, the quality of courage.

10. bribery: meaning, the act of influencing the act of another by a gift of money, like bribery of common man.

11. reformatory: meaning, a place, where the young wrongdoer is helped to reform.

12. repertory: meaning, a place where something may be placed or the plays presented in turn by a drama group.

ATE = CAUSE, MAKE

The following words can be formed from this particular root.

1. dedicate: meaning, t*o set apart for* a *purpose.*

2. advocate: meaning, to speak for or to defend.

3. arrogate: meaning, to claim as one's own without the right to do so.

4. educate: meaning, to provide with schooling or knowledge.

5. consecrate: meaning, to put into religious office by a rite or to make sacred, such as to consecrate an altar.

6. abbreviate: meaning, to m*ake short.*

7. deviate: meaning, to turn aside from the right way or to cause to stray.

8. attenuate: meaning, to make thin or to weaken.

9. enumerate: meaning, to count or list one after the other.

10. emanate: meaning, to come from or to flow forth.

11. exaggerate: meaning, to cause to appear larger than reality.

ANCE/ANCY=ACTION, PROCESS, QUALITY, STATE, DEGREE

The following words can be formed from this particular root.

1. accountancy: meaning, the job of record keeping.

2. assistance: meaning, the act of giving help to one who is in need of it.

3. attendance: meaning, the act of waiting upon or service.

4. allowance: meaning, the amount granted, often for expenses.

5. alliance: meaning, the state of being joined together.

6. defiance: meaning, the act of defying or the state of being against.

7. endurance: meaning, the ability to withstand hardship.

8. elegance: meaning, the qualities of tastefulness and gracefulness.

9. reluctance: meaning, *unwillingness.*

10. tolerance: meaning, an act of courteous forbearance to differences.

11. intolerance: meaning, opposite of an act of courteous forbearance to differences

12. militancy: meaning, a *fighting spirit.*

ENCE/ENCY = ACTION, STATE, QUALITY

This particular root is the same in meaning, as the previous root, but for a slight difference in the spelling. The following words can be formed from this particular root.

1. difference: meaning, the state, quality, or measure of being unlike.

2. competence: meaning, the quality of fitness or ability.

3. complacency: meaning, the state of smugness or self-satisfaction.

4. conference: meaning, the act of meeting within a group to exchange opinions.

5. deficiency: meaning, the state or quality of lacking something.

6. existence: meaning, *the quality of being.*

7. influence: meaning, the act of creating an impression or power.

8. obedience: meaning, an act of obeying, like obedience to the law

9. patience: meaning, the ability to wait or tolerate something.

10. opulence: meaning, the quality of having plenty, usually used for wealth or affluence.

11. proficiency: meaning, the state or quality of being skilled or an expert.

12. efficiency: meaning, the ability to get results.

BE = INTENSIVE

This particular root does not change the meaning, of the word. It just adds a certain richness to the word. The following words can be formed from this particular root.

1. bedeck: meaning, to cover up or to dress with finery.

2. bedight: meaning, to *adorn.*

3. beguile: meaning, to bewitch or to deceive.

4. behaviour: meaning, one's *manner or one's conduct.*

5. belabour: meaning, to beat severly or to thwack.

6. beleaguer: meaning, to block or to surround.

7. beloved: meaning, loved with great intensity.

8. bemused: meaning, carried away in a dream state.

9. benighted: meaning, to be overtaken by night or darkness.

10. bewail: meaning, to weep for, express great sorrow or to mourn.

11. behove: meaning, to be necessary or proper.

ISE = MAKE

Most of the words on this list can be converted to nouns by adding the suffix tion to them. The following words can be formed from this particular root.

1. acclimatise: meaning, to adapt to new conditions, as of soil.

2. cauterise: meaning, to sear with hot iron.

3. emphasise: meaning, to make important by putting stress upon.

4. familiarise: meaning, to make well-known.

5. pasteurise: meaning, to treat foods by Pasteur's method.

6. liberalise: meaning, to make free from narrow-mindedness.

7. mesmerise: meaning, to subject to hypnosis.

8. notarise: meaning, to make legal by signing before a notary.

9. idolise: meaning, to treat like an idol.

10. ostracise: meaning, to banish from society or to shun.

11. pauperise: meaning, to make very poor.

12. penalise: meaning, to subject to punishment.

13. publicise: meaning, to make the public aware of.

ANTE = BEFORE

This root should not be confused with the root ANTI, which means against. The words given below are actually Latin, but because they are so often used in English, they have become a part of English itself. The following words can be formed from this particular root.

1. antebellum: meaning, *existing before the war.*

2. antebrachium: meaning, the forearm.

3. antecede: meaning, to go before.

4. antecedent: meaning, anything happening or existing before another.

5. anteroom: meaning, a room before another.

6. antedate: meaning, to precede in time or to assign a date that is earlier than the actual date.

7. antediluvian: meaning, belonging to the time before the Biblical Flood.

8. anteflexed: meaning, bent forward.

9. antepast: meaning, a foretaste, like an appetizer.

10. antelucan: meaning, before dawn, like the meetings of the early Christians.

11. antenuptial: meaning, that which comes *before marriage.*

12. anterior: meaning, preceding in time or place.

13. antennae: meaning, the feelers on the head of an insect or used as organs of touch.

Part III

WORD BANK

This section will provide with a list of some uncommon words to help the reader enrich his vocabulary. Using the words frequently and bringing them in day-to-day conversation will help learn these words easily.

A

abstruse: hard to understand

accretion: increase by external growth

ACHILLES' HEEL: ATHLETE'S COMPLAINT

acolyte	:	an attendant
acrimony	:	bitterness
actuary	:	insurance expert
acumen	:	penetrating insight
affidavit	:	a written statement made on oath

aficionado	:	a keen fan or follower
agnostic	:	a person who denies knowledge of God
agronomy	:	study of grasses
akimbo	:	hands on hips with elbows bent outward
alfresco	:	a famous New York salad; fizzy Italian wines
alter ego	:	one's other self
amalgam	:	a compound of different metals
amanuensis	:	a secretary
ambidextrous	:	ability to use both hands with equal facility
ambivalent	:	being indecisive or having conflicting feelings towards a person or thing
amortise	:	to reduce or pay off a debt
anachronism	:	a person or event misplaced in time
analogous	:	similar in some respects
anathema	:	something hated; a person or a thing under a curse
angst	:	unfounded anger; anxiety
annul	:	cancel; to do away with
animus	:	hostility
anosmia	:	inability to smell
antipathy	:	strong aversion

antonym	:	a word of opposite meaning
aperient	:	laxative
aphorism	:	a short, pithy saying
apiarian	:	relating to bees
aplomb	:	poise and assurance
apocalyptic	:	ominous
apogee	:	highest or the farthest point
apposite	:	appropriate
apostasy	:	renouncing one's religion or principles

B

badinage	:	teasing banter and repartee
bacchanalian	:	riotous and drunken revelry
bakelite	:	a heat-resistant synthetic resin
baleful	:	having evil, deadly intention
balustrade	:	a banister supported by balusters
bar mitzvah	:	a Jewish ceremony for admitting a boy as an adult
baroque	:	extravagant style of decoration or architecture
bathos	:	a ridiculous change from ordinary or sublime condition

bayou	:	marshy, slow-running stream in America
beatitude	:	heavenly bliss
behemoth	:	a huge person, animal or object
bel canto	:	virtuoso singing
bellicose	:	aggressive or quarrelsome nature
bellwether	:	anything proposing direction of events or general tendency
bemused	:	bewildered and confused
benign	:	kindly, gentle and genial
besmirch	:	to make dirty
bibelot	:	a small but valuable article; a trinket
biennial	:	occurring every two years
bifurcate	:	to divide into two
bijou	:	a small, valuable jewel or trinket
bilateral	:	relating to two sides or parties
binary	:	system of numbers using 2 as its base
biopsy	:	removal of tissue from a body for examination
blasé	:	satiated or bored due to over-indulgence in pleasure
blench	:	to become pale

blithely	:	showing a cheerfully, carefree temperament
bona fide	:	genuinely, in good faith
bonhomie	:	good-natured friendliness
bon vivant	:	one who enjoys good food and drink
boreal	:	of the north
bourgeoisie	:	the middle classes
bowdlerise	:	to remove offensive words and passages from a book
braggadocio	:	noisy bragging, boasting
braise	:	to cook slowly in liquid in a closed pan
Brobdingnagian	:	of gigantic proportions.
brouhaha	:	a fuss, an uproar
brusque	:	blunt or rough in manner or speech
bucolic	:	relating to the countryside; of shepherds

C

cabal	:	a group of plotters
cabriole	:	a curved chair leg
caches	:	a hiding place for food, supplies, etc.
cajole	:	persuading with flattery

calcareous	:	containing calcium carbonate, calcium, or lime
callipygian	:	having well-formed buttocks
callisthenics	:	exercises for strength and beauty
calumny	:	a maliciously false statement
camaraderie	:	loyalty among comrades
campanology	:	the study of bell-ringing
canard	:	a false rumour
candour	:	being fair and open; the quality of integrity
cantankerous	:	disagreeable and crotchety
captious	:	hard to please; one who is fond of finding faults
carcanet	:	a jewelled collar
carpal	:	relating to the wrist
carte blanche	:	permission to act freely and unrestrained
cartel	:	an agreement between business interests to regulate output and prices
castellated	:	castle-like
castigate	:	to chastise
catalysis	:	to speed up a chemical reaction with a substance that remains unchanged
catamite	:	a boy prostitute

catharsis	:	purging emotional problems through dramatic re-enactment
catheter	:	a tube for draining fluids from the body
causerie	:	an informal conversation
caveat emptor	:	let the buyer beware
cavil	:	to find fault
celerity	:	swiftness
chancel	:	the area around the altar reserved for the clergy
charlatan	:	an imposter pretending to have expert knowledge or skill
chauvinism	:	blind patriotism
chiaroscuro	:	the visual effects of light and shade in painting, drawing, etc.
chicanery	:	trickery
chiffonier	:	a sideboard, usually with shelves and mirror alone
chimera	:	an imaginary monster or horror
choleric	:	bad-tempered
chutzpah	:	unabashed audacity
cinéaste	:	a serious movie enthusiast
circa	:	approximate

circumlocution	:	a roundabout or lengthy way of talking
circumscribed	:	to be restricted
clandestine	:	conducted in secrecy
clement	:	mild and gentle
cognoscenti	:	connoisseurs
colloquy	:	a dialogue, especially a formal conversation
collude	:	to conspire, usually for dishonest purposes
comity	:	friendliness
complaisant	:	eager to please
concomitant	:	in conjunction with
concupiscence	:	sexual lust
conflation	:	blending two things together
consanguinity	:	related by birth
contemn	:	to despise someone
contretemps	:	an awkward and embarrassing situation
corpus delicti	:	facts about a crime
coruscate	:	to glitter
costive	:	constipated
coterie	:	an exclusive group of people sharing common interests
crapulous	:	given to overindulgent drinking and eating

crescendo	:	a gradual increase in sound and force
cruciform	:	shaped like a cross
crustaceans	:	crabs and lobsters
cultivar	:	a plant originated by cultivation
cupidity	:	excessive desire to possess
cynosure	:	one who is centre of attraction
cytology	:	study of living cells

D

dado	:	lower part of the wall of a room when differently decorated from upper part
dalliance	:	flirting
dearth	:	scarcity
debacle	:	a complete rout and collapse
debilitate	:	to weaken
déclassé	:	having lost social status
declivity	:	a gradual slope downwards
de facto	:	existing, though, not legally
defalcate	:	to misappropriate money
defenestration	:	throwing someone out of a window
dégagé	:	free and easy in manner or attitude

déjà vu	:	the illusion of having previous experience of a present event
deleterious	:	noxious
delphic	:	ambiguous
demagoguery	:	emotional, prejudiced oratory
demotic	:	belonging to the common people
demurrer	:	an objection
dénouement	:	the unravelling and solution of a mystery
depilatory	:	for removing unwanted hair
de rigueur	:	required by etiquette
desiccate	:	to dry completely
desultory	:	casual and unmethodical
determinism	:	belief that external forces and not heredity determine an individual's actions and fate
dextral	:	right-handed
dialectic	:	logical and analytical argument
dichotomy	:	divided into two
didactic	:	inclined to teach
dilatory	:	slow
dipsomaniac	:	alcoholic
discommode	:	to take away a person's passport

discrete	:	detached and separate
disparage	:	depreciate or discredit
dissemble	:	to hide one's intentions
distrain	:	to seize goods in payment for a debt
diurnal	:	relating to daytime
divertissement	:	an entertainment
doctrinaire	:	dogmatic devotion to a theory
dolorous	:	full of pain and grief
double entendre	:	a risqué ambiguous statement
doughty	:	formidably brave
doyen	:	the senior member of a profession or group
draconian	:	harsh
drugget	:	a coarse woven mat
dudgeon	:	sullen resentment
duodenum	:	the first portion of the small intestine

E

ebullient	:	full of high spirits and enthusiasm
effulgent	:	shining brightly
egalitarian	:	one who believes in human equality
egocentric	:	self-centred
egregious	:	flagrantly appalling

élan	:	flamboyance
elegiac	:	melancholic and mournful
elephantine	:	huge, unwieldy
élite	:	the best
Elysian	:	blissful state, like a paradise
emanate	:	to issue or flow from
emancipate	:	to set free
emasculate	:	to weaken, to deprive of masculine properties
embargo	:	to ban or prohibit
embolism	:	the blocking of an artery or vein by a blood clot
embryonic	:	developing
emendate	:	to correct by removing errors and faults
emollient	:	a preparation that softens and soothes
emolument	:	a payment for services
empathy	:	understanding another's feelings
empirical	:	conclusions based on experiment, experience or observation
encomium	:	a citation of very high praise
endemic	:	found in a particular place; indigenous
enervate	:	to weaken
enfant terrible	:	an unmanageable child

engender	:	to cause or bring about something
enigma	:	something unexplainable
enjoin	:	to order or instruct someone to do something
ennui	:	listlessness and boredom
enormity	:	an atrocity of outrageous proportions
enunciate	:	to articulate clearly
ephemera	:	something short-lived or transitory
epicure	:	a person fond of sensual pleasures, especially eating and drinking
epigram	:	a witty saying or short verse
equitable	:	fair and just
equivocal	:	ambiguous, uncertain
ergonomics	:	the study of working conditions and efficiency
erogenous	:	sexually sensitive
ersatz	:	an artificial or inferior substitute
eructation	:	belching
erudite	:	well-read and well-informed
esoteric	:	something intelligible only to an initiated few

esprit de corps	:	spirit of loyalty and devotion to a group to which one belongs
ethos	:	the inherent characteristics of a culture or organisation
etymology	:	the origin and history of words
eugenics	:	the science of improving hereditary characterstics characteristics
eulogise	:	to praise highly
euphemism	:	the substitution of a bland or pleasant expression for a disagreeable one
euphoria	:	the heady feeling of supreme well-being
Eurasian	:	of mixed European and Asian blood
euthanasia	:	painless killing of terminally ill or old people
evanescent	:	fading away
exacerbate	:	to irritate and make worse
excoriate	:	to remove the skin
exculpate	:	to free from blame
execrable	:	detestable; of poorest quality
exegesis	:	a critical explanation or interpretation

exemplary	:	someone or something so good as to be worth imitating
exorcise	:	to drive out evil or evil spirits
expatiate	:	to speak or write at great length; elaborate or enlarge
expatriate	:	to expel someone from a country by force; exile
expiate	:	to atone or make amends
expropriate	:	to dispossess an owner of something, usually property, often for public use
expurgate	:	to remove supposedly offensive passages from a book etc.
extirpate	:	to exterminate; abolish

F

facile	:	something accomplished easily but without depth
factotum	:	a 'jack of all trades' sort of servant
fait accompli	:	an accomplished fact
fallacy	:	a false belief or argument
farrago	:	a confused mixture
fascism	:	authoritarian government
fastidious	:	hard to please
fatuous	:	complacently stupid
faux pas	:	a social indiscretion

fealty	:	loyalty
febrile	:	inclined to be feverish
feckless	:	a person without purpose or principles
fecund	:	fertile; productive
felicitous	:	charming and well-suited
feral	:	in a wild state
fervid	:	impassioned
filibuster	:	the technique of delaying the progress of legislation by prolonged speechmaking
flaccid	:	flabby
flews	:	the pendant jowls of certain breeds of dogs
flippant	:	frivolous
florescence	:	blossoming of a plant
florid	:	ruddy or highly embellished
flout	:	treat with contempt
foible	:	a personal weakness
forensic	:	pertaining to law courts
fortuitous	:	accidental
fractious	:	restless and irritable
friable	:	crumbly
fulgent	:	bright and dazzling
fulminate	:	to explode
fulsome	:	excessive and insincere

fundamentalism	:	belief in the literal truth of sacred texts
furbelow	:	showy trimming on clothing
furlough	:	leave of absence

G

gaffe	:	tactless remark or blunder
gambit	:	an opening move
gamut	:	a whole range
garrulous	:	talkative
gauche	:	awkward and socially graceless
gazebo	:	a small summer house with a view
gefilte fish	:	fish meal and eggs, shaped into balls
genuflect	:	to bend the knees
germane	:	relevant
gerrymander	:	manipulation of electoral boundaries to provide an unfair advantage to a candidate
gestation	:	the period from conception to birth
gesundheit	:	'Good Health!'
gigolo	:	a paid male escort
glutinous	:	sticky
gobbet	:	a lump or piece
gobbledegook	:	pompous jargon

gratuitous	:	uncalled for
gravamen	:	key point or essence of a legal action
gregarious	:	one who enjoys company
gumption	:	energetic initiative

H

habeas corpus	:	demand for a prisoner to appear before the court
habitué	:	a regular visitor
hackneyed	:	stale and trite
hagiography	:	a biography that regards its subject as a saint
ha-ha	:	a sunken fence
halcyon	:	peaceful and pleasant
halitosis	:	bad breath
hapless	:	unfortunate and unlucky
harbinger	:	someone or something that foretells an event
hector	:	to bully
hegemony	:	the dominance of one country over another
heinous	:	outrageously wicked
hellebore	:	a group of plants
heresy	:	an unorthodox belief
heterogeneous	:	of different kind

heuristic	:	the capacity to inquire and find out
hiatus	:	a break or gap
Hibernian	:	pertaining to Ireland
hindsight	:	wise after the event
histology	:	study of organic tissue
hogmanay	:	last day of the year
hoi polloi	:	common people
hologram	:	a three-dimensional photo-graphic image
homogeneous	:	all the same kind
honorarium	:	a payment
hortatory	:	giving encouragement
hubris	:	arrogant conceit or pride
humanism	:	a system concerned with the needs of man
humdrum	:	dull and tedious
hydrology	:	the study of water
hygrometer	:	measures moisture in the air
hyperbole	:	exaggeration

I

iconoclast	:	one who attacks established doctrines and beliefs
idiomatic	:	speech and expressions characteristic of a particular language.

idiosyncrasy	:	a personal habit or peculiarity of manner
idolatry	:	worship of idols and images
ignominy	:	disgrace and dishonour
imbroglio	:	a complex and confused state of affairs
immolate	:	to kill by sacrifice, usually by fire
immured	:	imprisoned, walled in
immutable	:	unchanging and unalterable
impasse	:	an insurmountable obstacle or situation
implacable	:	unrelenting and not to be appeased
importune	:	to demand urgently and persistently
imprimatur	:	a mark of approval
impromptu	:	off hand, without preparation
impugn	:	to dispute the validity or truth of an argument, or challenge the word of someone
inadvertent	:	unintentionally careless
incipient	:	in the first stages
incognito	:	avoiding recognition by disguise or by assuming another name
inculcate	:	to impress on the mind by repetition or force

incumbent	:	the holder of a position or office;
indemnity	:	security against damage or loss
indigenous	:	native to a particular country or region
indigent	:	destitute
ineffable	:	too overwhelming to be expressed in words
ineluctable	:	inevitable and unavoidable
inexorable	:	unmoved, unbending and unyielding
infra dig	:	beneath one's dignity
ingénue	:	a naive and artless young girl
ingenuous	:	open, candid and frank
inimical	:	hostile and behaving like an enemy
innate	:	inborn
innocuous	:	harmless
innuendo	:	an oblique hint or suggestion, usually derogatory
insalubrious	:	unhealthy
insidious	:	subtly intent on deceiving or betraying
insouciant	:	careless and unconcerned
inter alia	:	among other things
interdict	:	to authoritatively forbid
internecine	:	mutually destructive

interstice	:	a small space or crack between two things
intransigent	:	uncompromising and irreconcilable
intrinsic	:	essential, inherent
introvert	:	someone interested in his own thoughts, feelings and actions
inveigh	:	to denounce verbally
invidious	:	provoking anger and resentment
irascible	:	easily excited and angered
irrevocable	:	incapable of being revoked or repealed

J

jaundiced	:	a prejudicial attitude, especially due to jealousy, envy, etc.
jejune	:	immature, insipid and uninteresting
jeopardy	:	exposure to danger
jeremiad	:	a long lamentation
jettison	:	to throw things overboard
jihad	:	a crusade for or against a belief or faith
jingoism	:	aggressive patriotism; chauvinism

jocose	:	humorous and facetious
joie de junta	:	joy of being alive
junta	:	a ruling council
juvenescence	:	becoming young again
juxtapose	:	to place something against something else

K

karma	:	destiny
kibbutz	:	an Israeli community farm
kitsch	:	sentimental, garish or pretentious
kleptomaniac	:	obsessive thief
kosher	:	food prepared in accordance with Jewish dietary laws
kowtow	:	behaving in a servile manner
kudos	:	praise and credit

L

lachrymose	:	ready to weep
laconic	:	economical (of speech)
lacuna	:	a gap or blank
laity	:	laymen
laissez-faire	:	policy of non-intervention
lambent	:	softly flickering
lampoon	:	a satiric attack

languor	:	lack of energy and enthusiasm
largess	:	a generous gift, usually money
lascivious	:	lustful
latent	:	existing but not noticeable
lateral	:	towards the side
laudable	:	praiseworthy
legerdemain	:	sleight of hand
leitmotif	:	a recurring theme
lèse-majesté	:	high treason
lethargic	:	drowsy and apathetic
libido	:	the sexual drive
libretto	:	text of an opera or vocal work
licentious	:	sexually unrestrained
lionise	:	to treat someone as a celebrity
lissom	:	supple
locum tenens	:	a professional substitute
logorrhea	:	abnormal talkativeness
longueur	:	a long tedious passage in a book or play
loquacious	:	one who is fond of talking
lothario	:	a seducer of women
louche	:	shady and devious
lubricious	:	oily and lecherous
lugubrious	:	mournful
lumpen	:	deprived and degraded

M

macerate	:	to soften by soaking
machiavellian	:	unscrupulous scheming
macrocosm	:	a universal whole
magisterial	:	dictatorial
magnum opus	:	the greatest work of an artist, composer or writer
maladroit	:	awkward and clumsy
malaise	:	a vague feeling of uneasiness and discomfort
malapropism	:	misusing words
mal de mer	:	sea sickness
malfeasance	:	official misconduct
malthusian	:	The theory that populations will always outstrip the food supply unless checked
maudlin	:	foolishly and tearfully sentimental
maunder	:	to wander incoherently
mea culpa	:	'It is my fault'
megalomania	:	delusions of grandeur
megrim	:	a severe headache and depression
mélange	:	a mixture
melee	:	a confused fight
mellifluous	:	sweetly flowing
menage	:	a household

mendacious	:	prone to lying and deception
mendicant	:	a beggar
mephitic	:	offensive to the nose
meretricious	:	vulgarly attractive
metabolism	:	the bodily process that converts food to energy
métier	:	one's natural vocation
metronymic	:	a name or qualities derived from a maternal ancestor
micron	:	one-millionth of a metre
micturate	:	to urinate frequently
milieu	:	environment
millennium	:	period of one thousand years
minatory	:	threatening
misanthropy	:	hatred of mankind
miscegenation	:	racial interbreeding
misnomer	:	a mistaken or wrongly applied name
misogyny	:	hatred of women
mnemonic	:	a device to help the memory
moiety	:	a half share
moire	:	a wavy-patterned fabric
monograph	:	a treatise on a single subject
moratorium	:	a temporary suspension of an activity
moribund	:	coming to an end

mot juste	:	the perfectly fitting word or phrase
mufti	:	ordinary clothes worn by a serviceman off duty
mundane	:	ordinary and matter of fact
myocardiogram	:	a record of the muscular activity of the heart
myopia	:	short-sightedness

N

nadir	:	the lowest possible point
nascent	:	beginning to exist or develop
nebulous	:	vague and indistinct
necropsy	:	examination of a dead body
nefarious	:	wicked and evil
negus	:	a drink of wine, hot water, sugar and spices
nemesis	:	retributive justice
neologism	:	the coining of a new word or giving a new meaning to an existing word
neophyte	:	a novice or beginner
nephritis	:	inflammation of the kidneys
nepotism	:	favouring one's relatives, especially in relation to jobs and positions
nexus	:	something that joins or links

nihilism	:	a doctrine that holds that nothing has value or meaning, and rejects all traditional values, beliefs and institutions
noisome	:	offensive and disgusting, especially a smell
nonage	:	the period of legal minority
nonchalant	:	indifferent, calm and cool
non sequitur	:	an illogical conclusion or statement
nostrum	:	a quack medicine
nubile	:	a woman of marriageable age
nugatory	:	unimportant and not worth anything

☐

obdurate	:	stubborn
obeisance	:	a gesture of homage
obfuscates	:	to confuse or obscure
obloquy	:	abusive and reproachful language
obsequious	:	servile
obsolescent	:	becoming outdated
obstreperous	:	unruly and uncontrollable
obviate	:	to make unnecessary
occidental	:	a Westerner

occlude	:	to shut out
odium	:	hatred
odontologist	:	cares for the teeth
oenologist	:	an expert in wine and winemaking
oeuvre	:	the whole work of a writer or artist
oligarchy	:	a government controlled by a privileged few
omniscient	:	knowing everything
ossified	:	into bone
ostensibly	:	seemingly
ostentatious	:	pretentious and showy
osteopathy	:	treatment using massage and bone manipulation
otiose	:	useless and futile
outré	:	eccentric
overt	:	open and public

P

paediatrician	:	a specialist in children's diseases
palaver	:	a drawn-out discussion
palpable	:	evident and obvious
panacea	:	a universal remedy
panache	:	dash and verve
Panglossian	:	optimistic

panegyric	:	an elaborate and very nattering expression of praise
panjandrum	:	a self-important official
pantheism	:	the doctrine that the universe is a manifestation of God
paparazzi	:	tenacious freelance photographers of celebrities
paradigm	:	a model example
paragon	:	a model or pattern of excellence
parametre	:	variable constants used to determine a mathematical problem
paramour	:	the lover of a married man or woman
paranoia	:	delusions of persecution or grandeur
paraphrase	:	a restatement in different words, intended to clarify
pariah	:	a social outcast
part mutual	:	a betting system that divides the total stakes among the winners
parlous	:	perilous
parsimony	:	stinginess
parvenu	:	a newly rich social upstart
passé	:	behind the times

pastiche	:	a work that imitates the style of another
paterfamilias	:	male head of a household
pathogenic	:	capable of causing disease
patina	:	an oxidised layer
patisserie	:	a shop selling pastries
partial	:	pertaining to a person's country of birth
patrician	:	an aristocrat
Pecksniffian	:	a hypocrite who advocates moral behaviour but who acts otherwise
pectorals	:	chest muscles
pedagogue	:	a schoolteacher
pedantry	:	excessive attention to rules and details
peignoir	:	a woman's long, loose negligee or dressing gown
pejorative	:	disparaging and derogatory
pellucid	:	clear and transparent
percipient	:	quick to see and understand
peregrination	:	a journey
peremptory	:	decisive and final
perennial	:	lasting for a long period of time; everlastingly
perfunctory	:	careless and half-hearted
peripatetic	:	always travelling

periphrasis	:	roundabout speech or writing
pernicious	:	harmful
peroration	:	the summing up at the end of a speech
perquisite	:	unearned money or benefit
persiflage	:	frivolous banter
perspicacious	:	having the ability to understand things clearly
pertinacious	:	stubbornly persistent
philanderer	:	a womaniser
philistine	:	a person indifferent to the arts and learning
phlegmatic	:	stolidly calm and unexcitable
physiognomy	:	a person's facial features
picayune	:	petty and niggling
pied-à-terre	:	a temporary or secondary apartment
pinnate	:	having the shape and arrangement of a feather
pixilated	:	slightly dotty
placebo	:	a substance given in place of real medicine
plagiarism	:	stealing and using another's ideas, inventions or writings and passing them off as one's own work
plangent	:	a deep and resounding noise
platonic	:	spiritual and non-sensual

plebeian	:	common and vulgar
plenary	:	complete and absolute
plethora	:	superabundance
plutocracy	:	rule by the wealthy
podiatry	:	the treatment of disorders of the feet
poignant	:	penetrating and affecting
poltroon	:	a craven coward
polymath	:	a person versed in many areas of learning
potable	:	suitable for drinking
preciosity	:	excessive refinement of speech
predicate	:	to assert as a fact
predilection	:	a special liking
prehensile	:	capable of grasping
prescient	:	having foresight
prevaricate	:	to evade and mislead
prima facie	:	self-evident
probity	:	proven integrity
proclivity	:	a strong and natural tendency
prolapse	:	the downward displacement of an organ
prolix	:	tediously long-winded
propinquity	:	nearness
propitious	:	favourable
pro rata	:	in the same proportion

proscribe	:	to forbid
proselytise	:	to convert someone from one opinion or belief to another
prosthesis	:	replacement of a body part with an artificial substitute
protean	:	versatile and changeable
provenance	:	place of origin
prurient	:	inquisitive about the smutty and obscene
psychosomatic	:	physical disorder caused by or influenced by the emotions
puerile	:	silly and childish
puissant	:	powerful
pukka	:	genuine and reliable
pulchritude	:	physical beauty
pullulate	:	to breed rapidly
punctilious	:	paying strict attention to details of conduct
purlieus	:	the outskirts and boundaries of a neighbourhood
pusillanimous	:	timid and cowardly
putative	:	supposed or reputed
putti	:	the naked cherubs in art and sculpture
Pyrrhic victory	:	a victory that is costly and fruitless

Q

quasi	:	having the semblance of
querulous	:	of a complaining disposition
quiddity	:	the essence or trifling uniqueness of something
quidnunc	:	a a busybody
quietus	:	release from life
quixotic	:	possessing high but impractical aims
quondam	:	former
quorum	:	an agreed number of people required to be present before a meeting can be held
quotidian	:	occurring daily

R

Rabelaisian	:	coaresely humorous, sarcastic, etc.
raconteur	:	an expert story-teller
raffish	:	flashy and disreputable
raillery	:	good-natured teasing
raison d'etere	:	reason for existing
rancour	:	deep-seated hatred and resentment
rapport	:	harmonious relationship

rapprochement	:	restoration of friendly relations after some disagreement
rara avis	:	someone or something very unusual
ratiocination	:	reasoning by the use of logic
raucous	:	harsh-sounding
reactionary	:	a person advocating change or progress
rebarbative	:	repellent and forbidding
recalcitrant	:	stubborn and uncontrollable
recant	:	to formally retract a belief or opinion
recherché	:	rare, strange and exquisite
recidivism	:	habitual relapse into criminal behaviour
recondite	:	obscure, profound and little-known
recrudesce	:	to break out afresh
rectitude	:	moral integrity
redolent	:	smelling of something that stirs the memory
redoubtable	:	formidable and commanding respect
referendum	:	a vote by the electorate to ratify or reject a particular issue
refractory	:	resistant and troublesome

refulgent	:	shining brightly
renege	:	break a promise or fail to fulfil an undertaking
reprehend	:	to criticise or blame
repudiate	:	to reject and disown
retrograde	:	to go backwards; deteriorate
retroussé	:	turned up at the tip
rhetorical	:	concerned with effect rather than content
rictus	:	a gaping open mouth
riparian	:	pertaining to river banks
riposte	:	a quick and clever reply
risible	:	inclined to laughter
rococo	:	highly elaborate and florid 18th-century French style of decoration
roué	:	a dissipated lecher
rumbustious	:	boisterous and unruly

S

salacious	:	obscene and lustful
salient	:	highly conspicuous
salutary	:	beneficial
sang-froid	:	coolness and composure under pressure
sardonic	:	sneering and scornful
Sassenach	:	an English person

saturnine	:	melancholic
savoir-faire	:	having a fine sense of what's right and wrong socially
Scaramouch	:	a boastful buffoon
scatology	:	an unhealthy interest in excrement
Schadenfreude	:	delight in another's misfortunes
scintilla	:	the tiniest, most minute particle
scrivener	:	a clerk who writes up documents
scut	:	a rabbit's tail
sebaceous	:	fatty
secular	:	pertaining to worldly things
sedulous	:	persistent and diligent
semantics	:	concerned with the meanings of words
semiotics	:	the study of signs in communications
senescent	:	growing old
sententious	:	pompous moralising
sequestered	:	secluded
serendipitous	:	the inclination to find things unexpectedly
serrated	:	saw-toothed
shibboleth	:	a password
sibilant	:	the sound of a hiss

silviculture	:	forestry
similitude	:	resemblance
simony	:	trading in sacred objects
simulacrum	:	a shadowy, deceptive likeness
sinecure	:	a well-paid cushy position
sinistral	:	left-handed
skulk	:	to lurk unseen with wrong-doing in mind
sobriquet	:	a nickname
soi-disant	:	'self-styled'
soigné	:	elaborately well-groomed
soiree	:	an evening of conversation and music
solecism	:	a grammatical mistake
solipsism	:	the theory that only the self is real and knowable
sommelier	:	a wine waiter
somnambulism	:	sleepwalking
sonorous	:	giving out a full, rich sound
sophistry	:	the use of fallacious and deceptive argument
soporific	:	sleep-inducing
sotto	:	voce in an undertone
spavined	:	worn out and broken down
specious	:	seemingly right and correct but actually not
splenetic	:	bad-tempered

sporadic	:	occurring occasionally
stasis	:	a static state
stentorian	:	loud and powerful
stultify	:	to make something appear foolish and absurd
stygian	:	impenetrably dark
subliminal	:	something perceived below the threshold of consciousness
subsume	:	to include or absorb into
succinct	:	sharp and concise
supercilious	:	arrogantly indifferent
supernumerary	:	superfluous
suppurate	:	to fester
surrogate	:	an appointed substitute
svelte	:	superbly groomed
sybaritic	:	a worshipper of Satan
sycophantic	:	servile
symbiosis	:	mutually advantageous partnership of two dissimilar organisms
synergy	:	co-operative activity to produce enhanced benefits
syntax	:	the rules of grammar that arrange the words in a sentence

T

tachometre	:	speed of rotation
tacit	:	implied
tactile	:	relating to sense of touch
talisman	:	a charm
tangible	:	real
taupe	:	grey-brown
telekinesis	:	ability to move things without touching them
temerity	:	boldness
temporal	:	earthly
temporise	:	to delay
tendentious	:	biased
tenet	:	a belief
tenuous	:	flimsy
tercentenary	:	an anniversary of 300 years
tessellated	:	chequered
theism	:	belief in one God
thrall	:	bondage
timorous	:	fearful
tinnitus	:	ringing in the ears
tocsin	:	an alarm
torpid	:	sluggish
tort	:	a private or civil wrong
tractable	:	docile
traduce	:	to defame

tranche	:	a portion
transcend	:	to rise beyond
transient	:	fleeting
travail	:	a painful toil
tremulous	:	trembling
trenchant	:	cutting and forceful
trichology	:	study of hair
tridactyl	:	having three fingers or toes
triptych	:	a painting on three panels
triumvirate	:	a group of three people wielding power
troglodyte	:	a cave dweller
trope	:	a figure of speech
truncate	:	to cut off the top
tumescent	:	becoming swollen
turbid	:	cloudy
turpitude	:	inherent depravity
tyro	:	a beginner

U

ubiquitous	:	existing everywhere
ullage	:	the space in a container not taken up by its contents
ululate	:	to howl or wail
umbrage	:	a sense of slight or injury
unconscionable	:	going beyond reasonable bounds

unctuous	:	oily and smasmy
unilateral	:	something done or undertaken by a single or party
urbane	:	polite and polished
usurious	:	extortionate interest on loans
uxorious	:	excessive doting on a wife

V

vacillate	:	to waver or sway to and fro
valetudinarian	:	a chronic invalid
vapid	:	insipid, dull and flat
venal	:	unprincipled and ready to accept bribe
vendetta	:	a long-lasting blood-feud
veracity	:	honesty and truthfulness
verbatim	:	word for word
vernacular	:	the native language, habits or activities
vernal	:	relating to spring
vertiginous	:	whirling round at a dizzy rate
vicarious	:	experienced or imagined through the words or deeds of another

W

wagon-lit	:	a sleeping car on a continental train dried and shrivelled
Wigened	:	dried and Shrivelled
wraith	:	a ghostly apparition of a living person or someone who has just died
wrangler	:	a person who argues in a quarrelsome way.
wunderkind	:	a child prodigy

X, Y, Z

xanthic	:	yellowish
yahoo	:	brutish half-human creature
yashmak	:	the veil worn by Muslim women in public
zealot	:	a fanatic
Zeitgeist	:	the spirit of an age
zenith	:	the highest point
ziggurat	:	a terraced, pyramidal temple
zwieback	:	a type of sweet cake

Part IV

WHY USE A DICTIONARY?

Dictionaries can be used to check spelling, to learn new words, to find or double-check the meaning of a word you encounter, or to find the right word to use. How to best use a dictionary depends on what you are doing with words. The use of dictionary differs:

- If you are a lawyer
- If you are a teacher
- If you are a student
- If you are learning English
- If you are learning another language
- When you are surfing the web
- When someone uses a word you do not understand
- When you are writing
- And finally, to avoid looking stupid

IF YOU ARE A LAWYER

Judges quote from the dictionary all the time. It is well known that the Supreme Courts increasingly cite dictionaries in their decisions. Many different dictionaries get cited. There is no single best dictionary. When preparing a brief, make sure that you look up key terms and refer to their definition. If a key term has multiple meanings, then use a thesaurus to find the correct unambiguous term.

A major part of legal research is sitting down in front of a search engine to find case law. A good dictionary lets you check the spelling of words before you launch a search. And a thesaurus lets you find synonyms and other related words.

IF YOU ARE A TEACHER

A dictionary has a number of features that benefit the learner of English at several levels. The dictionary means that the teacher is not forced to analyse each word to see whether each learner is familiar with the use of a word in a specific context. The ability to use a slightly more advanced vocabulary, without risk, reinforces the existing vocabulary for those who have seen it and allows others to rapidly acquire the vocabulary, giving them the confidence to take on more challenging texts. The value of this risk-free uncertainty, certainly, depends on the cultural importance of embarrassment for the learner.

The active acquisition of vocabulary, by selecting a word and using it, engages the student and reinforces the learning process more than a passive glossary. Further, by presenting several senses the process of selecting the correct word introduces the cognitive process of disambiguation that the reader having a larger vocabulary needs to acquire. Out of all the possible meanings, the learner must pick the correct one, therefore, moving from a lexical to a semantic understanding of the term within the text.

IF YOU ARE A STUDENT

How do you look up the spelling of a word when you do not know how it is spelled? Start out your research on any paper with a dictionary. It will get you keywords, phrases and synonyms that will help you formulate your understanding of the word and its use.

It is good to have a dictionary handy, when you are reading a document. If you are unsure of the meaning of a word in a document, you just highlight the word and can later, on look for its meaning in the dictionary.

How about if the definition of a word uses a word you do not understand? Once again, browse through the dictionary. Though it can be exhausting, but this will only increase your vocabulary.

IF YOU ARE LEARNING ENGLISH

A dictionary is a great companion to stretch a small vocabulary. When you come across a word, you are not familiar with, a dictionary helps you by defining the word and giving you examples of its use in a sentence. If you hear the word, rather than reading it, you may not be sure how to spell it. This is where a dictionary can help. If you read the word, your may be faced with an irregular plural or participle. For instance, if you see the word 'spoken' you need to look up the word 'speak'.

While you are looking up the word, you have an opportunity to learn a number of related words. The word may have several meanings. The more you learn English, the greater the number of secondary meanings you want to look up. These are usually in order of how commonly the sense is used. The better your English, the more senses you want to become familiar with. This will avoid confusion in the future as you start reading more complex documents. It is also useful to look up synonyms while you are there. Looking up synonyms is a good way of confirming that you have actually understood the word. Are the synonyms listed by the dictionary interchangeable in a sentence with the word you are looking up? If not, you may have the wrong sense of the word.

Another great tool for increasing vocabulary is learning 'related terms'. You can look up more general or more specific terms. Looking up more general terms is great for reading, as it helps better understand the word.

You can look up a similar or related word, or a general word, and by following the links you can find the right word. For instance, i1f you are looking for a word that means to see something quickly, you can look up the word 'see', then find more specific terms like 'get a look' or its synonym 'catch a glimpse'.

Another way of using a dictionary is to translate a term into your language. There are a number of online dictionaries, which take a word in English and translate it into your language, or vice-versa.

WHEN YOU ARE WRITING

A dictionary is an essential tool for writers. You have to make sure that words are spelled correctly. It is a good habit to vary your vocabulary. This means that you should not use the same word too many times in a row. When you see, you are about to use the same word again, look it up in the thesaurus.

TO AVOID LOOKING STUPID

Some people use fancy words to stifle open discussion, particularly in meetings. Or you may be new to a field and willing to learn and for any word there is always a first time. Psychologists will tell you that one of the major motivators in life is to avoid looking stupid. If you actually are stupid, then no dictionary will help you. But if you are not, an online dictionary or the traditional one is a good way to quickly and discreetly bring yourself to speed on the vocabulary that others are using.

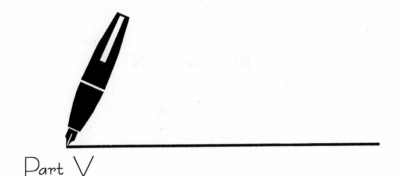

Part V

WORD GAMES

Word games are not just fun, but also play an important part in boosting one's vocabulary. Below are given a few games that will help you increase your word bank!

GAME 1

See if by changing only one letter at a time, you change the first word to the second?

(A)

W	A	R	N
L	O	N	E

(B)

M	A	N
P	U	P

(C)

S	O	R	E
Y	A	R	D

Game 2

The words in the grid begin and end with 'L'. Match them with their meanings and fill in the grid.

CLUES

1. part of coat front.
2. deadly
3. generous
4. pea
5. legal
6. slander
7. tag
8. true
9. exact, word for word
10. regional

Literal

Lawful

Libel

Loyal

Lentil

Local

Lapel

Liberal

Lethal

Label

GAME 3

The third complete column down forms half of a proverb. Fill in the grid and then write out the first half of the following proverb

"_____ run deep"

1. face covering

1. slant

3. cut off

4. a friend

5. opposite of short

6. not fast

7. an insect

8. a plot

9. the colour of grass

10. game

11. type or kind

1. face covering
2. slant
3. cut off
4. a friend
5. opposite of short
6. not fast
7. an insect
8. a plot
9. the colour of grass
10. game
11. type or kind

GAME 4

Match things with their descriptions:
1. knife: (a) a thing for taking pictures
2. soap: (b) used for shaving
3. shaving cream (c) used for washing
4. camera: (d) used for keeping money
5. pencil (e) used for stitching
6. sewing machine (f) used for adding
7. calculator (g) used for cutting
8. shoes(h) used for sticking
9. gum(i) used for writing
10. handbag(j) used for walking

GAME 5

Fill in the blanks, forming a new word from the highlighted word:

1. It was not _____ after all, merely a **pastromi** overdose.

2. He _____, "I'm the best!," as he **outsped** the rest.

3. He is even _____ when he is **rewired** on coffee.

4. He **misrates** motels, using an _____ instead of an asterisk.

5. He is _____ the soil by **breaking** it.

6. His chute was faulty _____ so his life was **briefed**.

7. She prayed for _____ from the **pestier** guest.

8. "Put an _____ next to your name, if you're so special," he said in the **sarkiest** manner.

9. The _____ minded are kin to the **doomily** disposed.

10. There are two sides to every story that the **verbose** tell: so _____ the **obverse** as well.

11. The tennist said, "You _____, I **deduce**!"

12. This _____ delves into **dustier** books.

13. There is an **inequity** between _____ and bovinity.

14. Some seem soft-spoken but those more _____ make their points with **tridents**.

15. _____ contains the **entirety** of time.

16. The artist sees _____fields as a **framable** scene.

17. Cats finish their nine lives **finitely**, yet with _____.

18. It was his _____ assumption that **groundsels** would sell.

19. He lost his **marbles**. That's why he _____.

20. He **mispled** his innocence on account of his _____.

GAME 6

Solve the following clues, giving another word for them. For example, Calculator - **abacus**

1. textile
2. failure to be present
3. exercise type
4. hot sauce
5. a muscle or a seizer
6. patient vehicle
7. tuna-type
8. like fables
9. more than enough

GAME 7

One clue (in each set of 3) defines a word of 5 or more letters. The other two clues define smaller words created using alternate letters starting at either the first or second letter of the larger word.

Example: eloquent, merriment, allow = fluent, fun (FlUeNt), let (fLuEnT) The clues below are in a less convenient (random) order. Form the words:

1. thwarted, interjection showing disapproval, antediluvian
2. un-even, compete, declared invalid
3. regret, theatrical group, acme
4. hurt, common conjunction, bakery treat
5. Adam's wife, belonging to us, writer's output
6. joined by treaty or agreement, heavy beer, hinged cover
7. broadcast, bee house, remuneration
8. succulent plant, light-haired, became inflated
9. aged, act in unison, evidence that helps solve a problem.
10. written records, raised platform, anger

GAME 8

This is a Geography word search game. The following words are present in the given grid of characters. You simply have to trace the words in the grid:

ABUDHABI, ADEN, AMMAN, ARABEMIRATES, BAGHDAD, BAHRAIN, BEIRUT, DAMASCUS, IRAN, IRAQ, ISRAEL, JERUSALEM, JORDAN, KUWAIT, KUWAITCITY, LEBANON, MANAMA, RIYADH,

SANA, SAUDIARABIA, SOUTHYEMEN, SYRIA, TEHRAN, YEMEN.

```
S O U T H Y E M E N Y G L G E
X A R A B E M I R A T E S F T
F M U U R Y Z G M Q I U Q I J
H H O D L O Y E R L C W A O F
U P D K I B L I P S T N R R X
W U X N I A R H A B I D I G X
R O V Y S B R M D W A R Y M W
O V J U D U A A G N W J A W L
L E R L N D D N B Y U S D N X
S E K T E H R A N I K K H V D
J T B N G A M M A N A S V N K
F A M A J B R A E S Z I L Q Q
K T B E N I A S R Y V J R V B
R K F Q E O B E I R U T M Y K
B E Z W H W N A P S E S A G S
```

GAME 9

Test your vocabulary skills on the following list of animal collectives. Match each animal with its appropriate collective noun.

bale, brace, cast, cete, charm, cloud, clutter, colony, congregation, covey, crash, drift, exaltation, gang, grist, husk, knot, leap, murder, muster, siege, skein, sleuth, volery, watch

1. _____ of ants

2. _____ of badgers

3. _____ of bears

4. _____ of bees

5. _____ of birds

6. _____ of cats

7. _____ of cranes

8. _____ of crows

9. _____ of ducks

10. _____ of elks

11. _____ of geese

12. _____ of gnats

13. _____ of goldfinches

14. _____ of hares

15. _____ of hawks

16. _____ of larks

17. _____ of leopards

18. _____ of nightingales

19. _____ of peacocks

20. _____ of plovers

21. _____ of quail

22. _____ of rhinoceri

23. _____ of swine

24. _____ of toads

25. _____ of turtle

GAME 10

Match each tradesman (using his surname as guide) with the object(s) of his work.

wagon, bow, cask, planks, kettle, arrows, candles

1. Mr. Cooper was applying a hoop to the _____ for Turner.

2. Mr. Bowyer was softening the wood required to fashion a(n) _____ for Glim.

3. Mr. Wheelwright was putting finishing touches on the _____ for Kerf.

4. A bored Mr. Sawyer was loading _____ on Stew's wagon.

5. The itinerant Mr. Tinker could be heard fixing Slat's _____.

6. Mr. Fletcher looked at his quiver, as he just received a large order for _____ from Archie.

7. The drippy Mr. Chandler was inspecting his latest batch of _____, ordered by Shaft.

GAME 11

Match up the words in the first column with its closest definition in column two.

___ tenacious   A. in a state of repair suitable for lease.

___ tenantable   B. sinewy.

___ tendentious   C. gloomy; dark.

___ tendinous   D. thin; slender; rare.

___ tenebrous   E.   sensuous; lascivious.

___ tenesmus   F.   a painful but ineffectual effort to urinate or defecate.

___ tentative   G. cohesive; tough; persistent.

___ tentiginous   H. biased.

___ tenuis   I. an unaspirated voiceless stop

___ tenuous   J. by way of experiment or trial.

GAME 12

Select the definition that best fits each word.

1. **minatory**

   a) threatening

   b) confined in a labyrinth

   c) algebraically negative

   d) capable of being mined

2. **ineffable**

   a) unavoidable

   b) unfriendly; uneasy in conversation

   c) indescribable

   d) apochryphal; of doubtful authenticity

3. **bumptious**

   a) unsophisticated; rustic

   b) serendipitous

   c) inclined to demote (one's employees)

   d) self-assertive; forward

4. **sonorous**

   a) loud-sounding

b) filled with something (as honey) that sweetens

c) producing a regular and monotonous ringing

d) non-conducting

5. **piquant**

a) stimulating to the taste

b) trivial

c) drawing attention

d) a two-handed card game played with 32 cards

6. **necromancer**

a) spectral diffuser

b) nocturnal bloodsucker

c) sorcerer

d) 3-D virtual environment

7. **effusion**

a) pouring a liquid on (as in a baptism)

b) the act of pouring out

c) joining by melting together

d) ostentatious show; gala

GAME 13

Match each word with its closest definition below:

___ arboretum

___ caryatid

___ coloratura

___ colporteur

___ demesne

___ dressage

___ intaglio

___ pithecanthropus

___ prophylactic

___ sidereal

___ xebec

___ zephyr

___ zwieback

a. sweetened bread that is baked and then sliced and toasted until dry and crisp.

b. a gentle breeze.

c. preventing or guarding from disease.

d. measured by the apparent motion of the fixed stars.

e. manorial land possessed by the lord and not held by free tenants.

f. the execution by a horse of complex maneuvers in response to barely perceptible movements of a rider's hands, legs, and weight.

g. a place where trees and plants are grown for scientific and educational purposes.

h. a sculptured draped female figure used as an architectural column.

i. a usu. 3-masted Mediterranean sailing ship with long overhanging bow and stern.

j. a peddler of religious books.

k. florid ornamentation in vocal music.

l.   an engraving or incised figure in a hard material (as stone) depressed below the surface of the material.

m.   any of several primitive extinct men from Java.

GAME 14

CROSS WORD

Clues to the 12 words

Session #136 - Level One Crossword

ACROSS:

- 2 - Usually a small, relatively inexpensive, article kept as a reminder

- 5 - Behaviour not conforming to prevailing laws

- 7 - To point out or demonstrate

- 11 - An exciting or unusual experience; a usually risky undertaking

- 12 - A particular state of being; a restricting circumstance

DOWN:

- 1 - Brought down to a smaller size, amount or price

- 3 - A book with the words of a language, usually arranged alphabetically

- 4 - A formal personal presentation of one person to another

- 6 - Not easily accessible or at hand ; not suiting one's needs

- 8 - Tending to instruct, inform or impart knowledge

- 9 - To originate as a product of one's own ingenuity

- 10 - Any judgment or decision; the findings of a jury

GAME 15

CHOOSE THE APPROPRIATE DEFINITION FOR EACH WORD

1. CARMAGNOLE

A. A lively song often accompanied by street dancing, popular during the French Revolution.

B. A disease of the liver that is in many cases terminal.

C. A type of derby that was worn in the late nineteenth century and originated in England.

2. SPATUNG

A. A sea urchin.

B. A snow crab.

C. A shrewish woman.

3. NAUTCH

A. A waterproof watch that is safe at great depths undersea.

B. A type of ancient hut.

C. A chorus line in India of nautch girls.

4. MANTELET

A. A small shelf above a fireplace.

B. A bulletproof screen.

C. A Norwegian soldier.

5. SARDOODLEDUM

A. A gadfly

B. A type of radish

C. A melodrama

6. MAHOUT

A. A metal boomerang with extremely sharp edges.

B. A prehistoric reptile with pointed tusks.

C. An elephant driver.

7. CAMISOLE

A. A container used to carry water or wine over long distances.

B. A short sleeveless garment for women.

C. A boastful, swaggering person.

8. LAGAN

A. Short, thin, diagonally cut tubular pasta.

B. A special gift or donation.

C.   Goods thrown into the sea with a buoy attached so that they may be found again.

9. CYMATIUM

A.   A crowning molding in classic architecture.

B.   The angle between an aircraft supporting surface (as a wing) and a horizontal transverse line.

C.   A small chamber or cavity especially in a plant or animal body.

10. HOPLITE

A.   A circle dance of Romania and Israel.

B.   A heavily armed infantry soldier of ancient Greece.

C.   A spittoon.

11. PRETERIST

A.   An architectual housing model.

B.   An appetizer.

C.   A person who enjoys reliving past memories.

12. PIGNUS

A.   The waning light from a flickering flame.

B.   Someone who enjoys language games.

C.   Property held as collateral against a debt.

13. NICTITATE

A.   A very wealthy man.

B.   Medical treatment using aloe and other healing herbs.

C.   To flirt by winking the eye.

14. THESICLE

A.   A type of one-horse sleigh.

B.   A small thesis or proposition.

C.   A variety of Asian buzzard.

15. GAWF

A.   A shiny red apple.

B.   A laugh that is accompanied by coughing.

C.   A slow burning fuse that is used in underground explosions.

16. SCHESIS

A.   A variety of skunk.

B.   That which sometimes follows Synthesis in a Hegelian model.

C.   To make fun of people's accents and mannerisms.

17. KINNIKINNIK

A. A gambling game played with three small cups and a ball.

B. A young palm tree.

C. Indian smoking substance made from tree bark.

18. SINDON

A. The tissue between the front and back legs of a flying squirrel that aids in flight.

B. A poisonous weed.

C. A book cover made of linen.

19. YASHMAK

A. An Indian biscuit.

B. An intense argument.

C. A face-veil worn by women of Moslem countries.

20. KILHIG

A. Dysentery.

B. In logging, a short pole used to direct the way a tree will fall.

C. As sharp as nails.

GAME 16

CROSS WORD PUZZLE

Clues to the 12 words:

Session #136 - Level Two Crossword

Across:

- 1 - A form of government where an imperious ruler has absolute power
- 3 - Involving the expression of the opposite opinion
- 7 - Full of incidents or important occurrences
- 9 - Artificial channel for conducting water over a distance
- 10 - Something that foretells the future; a prophecy
- 11 - The act of stopping or keeping something from happening

Down:

- 1 - To devote wholly to some action (past tense)
- 2 - Capable of creating by mental or physical effort; yielding favourable results
- 4 - To infer; to derive as a conclusion from something known or assumed
- 5 - Showing a disposition to undertake something involving risk
- 6 - A woman who holds the title of duke in her own right
- 8 - Conforming to accepted standards (conduct or taste)

GAME 17

Match up the collective noun with the appropriate animal(s):

___ bevy	A.	a school of marine mammals, such as seals, whales, or dolphins.
___ covey	B.	a flock of geese or similar birds in flight.
___ nide	C.	a family or small flock of birds, especially partridge or quail.
___ pod	D.	herd of wild boar
___ skein	E.	a nest or brood of pheasants
___ skulk	F.	a group of animals or birds, especially larks or quail.
___ sounder	G.	a congregation of vermin, especially foxes.

GAME 18

Match up each term with the appropriate definition below:

___ axilla	A:	The space between the eyebrows, just above the nose.
___ canthus	B:	The pendent fleshy lobe in the middle of the posterior border of the soft palate.
___ frenum	C:	Pertaining to the throat

___	glabella	D:	The corner where the upper and under eyelids meet on each side of the eye.
___	gular	E.	The armpit, or the cavity beneath the junction of the arm and shoulder.
___	lunula	F:	A connecting fold of membrane serving to support or restrain any part; as of the tongue
___	uvula	G:	The crescent-shaped area at the base of the human fingernail

GAME 19

Match the word with its best definition below:

___	samson	1.	a very wise man.
___	solomon	2.	one who proffers some illusory advantage or benefit.
___	vandal	3.	one who willfully destroys or defaces any work of art or literature.
___	hegira	4.	mistress; a sweetheart.
___	barmecide	5.	an impostor in argument; a captious or fallacious reasoner.
___	dulcinea	6.	a man of extraordinary physical strength.
___	sophist	7.	any flight or exodus regarded as like that of Mohammed.

GAME 20

Choose a word for the highlighted word or the blank:

1.   He **looked** at his watch quickly.
     a. searched
     b. reached
     c. glanced
     d. sobbed
     e. raced

2.   The robbers **looked through** the whole house for money.
     a. searched
     b. glanced
     c. hunted
     d. sobbed
     e. tossed

3.   When she got her test back, she was so disappointed that she **threw** it away.
     a. searched
     b. poured
     c. roared
     d. tossed
     e. raced

4.   The waiter **put** Kuala Beer into my glass.
     a. filled
     b. poured
     c. reached

d. threw

e. tossed

5. When her dog died, she **cried very hard** for half an hour.

a. yelled

b. screamed

c. sobbed

d. raced

e. drowned

6. It was foggy and I watched my friend **move out of sight** into the distance as he walked away.

a. toss

b. throw

c. disappear

d. pour

e. race

7. Would you like some more to eat. No thank you. I've had **more than enough** already.

a. amount

b. race

c. pour

d. plenty

e. much

8. This road **turns a lot**.

a. races

b. roars

c. admits

d. widens

e. bends

9. Please do this **now**!

a. immediately

b. later

c. sooner

d. whenever

e. before long

10. Someone who is not strong is ___ .

a. muscular

b. weak

c. pale

d. raced

e. excited

11. When your face does not have much colour, it is ___

a. pale

b. excited

c. calm

d. seek

e. painted

12. Another word for quiet is ___ .

a. excited

b. adventure

c. pale

    d. calm

    e. search

13. A story from the past is called a ___ .

    a. account

    b. article

    c. exciting

    d. myth

    e. ancient

14. On a clear night, the moon ___ so brightly that you can see your shadow.

    a. pours

    b. shines

    c. excites

    d. looks

    e. seems

15. A box for keeping valuable things is called a ___

    a. valuable

    b. mommy

    c. plenty

    d. safe

    e. sale

Answers

Game 1

(A) war, ward, word, lord, lore, lone.

(B) Man, pan, pat, pit, pip, pup.

(C) Sore, core, corn, born, barn, yarn, yard

GAME 2

1. lapel
2. lethal
3. liberal
4. lentil
5. lawful
6. libel
7. label
8. loyal
9. literal
10. local

GAME 3

1. mask
2. tilt
3. snip
4. pal
5. tall
6. slow
7. gnat
8. site
9. green

10. sport

11. class

"still waters run deep"

GAME 4

1. g

2. c

3. b

4. a

5. i

6. e

7. f

8. j

9. h

10. d.

GAME 5

1. atropism   2. spouted   3. weirder

4. asterism   5. breaking   6. fibered

7. respite   8. asterisk   9. moodily

10. observe   11. deuced   12. studier

13. equinity   14. strident   15. eternity

16. farmable   17. felinity   18. groundless

19. rambles   20. dimples

GAME 6

1. fabric
2. absence
3. aerobic
4. Tabasco
5. abductor
6. ambulance
7. albacore
8. parabolic
9. abundance

GAME 7

1. FOILED, FIE, OLD
2. VOIDED, VIE, ODD
3. TROUPE, TOP, RUE
4. PAINED, PIE, AND
5. OEUVRE, OUR, EVE
6. ALLIED, ALE, LID
7. APIARY, AIR, PAY
8. BALLOONED, BLOND, ALOE
9. COLLUDE, CLUE, OLD
10. DIARIES, DAIS, IRE

GAME 8

(Over, Down, Direction)

ABUDHABI(6,6,S)

ADEN(7,8,SW)

AMMAN(6,11,E)

ARABEMIRATES(2,2,E)

BAGHDAD(3,13,NE)

BAHRAIN(10,6,W)

BEIRUT(7,14,E)

DAMASCUS(6,9,NE)

IRAN(11,6,SE)

IRAQ(13,6,N)

ISRAEL(9,14,NW)

JERUSALEM(1,11,NE)

JORDAN(15,3,SW)

KUWAIT(11,10,N)

KUWAITCITY(11,10,N)

LEBANON(1,9,SE)

MANAMA(8,7,S)

RIYADH(13,5,S)

SANA(12,11,W)

SAUDIARABIA(1,1,SE)

SOUTHYEMEN(1,1,E)

SYRIA(15,15,NW)

TEHRAN(4,10,E)

YEMEN(6,1,E)

GAME 9

1. a *colony* of ants
2. a *cete* of badgers
3. a *sleuth* of bears
4. a *grist* of bees
5. a *volery* of birds
6. a *clutter* of cats
7. a *siege* of cranes
8. a *murder* of crows
9. a *brace* of ducks
0. a *gang* of elks
11. a *skein* of geese
12. a *cloud* of gnats
13. a *charm* of goldfinches
14. a *husk* of hares
15. a *cast* of hawks
16. an *exaltation* of larks
17. a *leap* of leopards
18. a *watch* of nightingales
19. a *muster* of peacocks
20. a *congregation* of plovers
21. a *covey* of quail
22. a *crash* of rhinoceri
23. a *drift* of swine
24. a *knot* of toads

25.   a *bale* of turtles

GAME 10

1. cask
2. a bow
3. wagon
4. planks
5. kettle
6. arrows
7. candles

GAME 11

tenacious – G
tenantable - A
tendentious - H
tendinous – B
tenebrous – C
tenesmus – F
tentative – J
tentiginous – E
tenuis – I
tenuous – D

GAME 12

1.   threatening

2. indescribable
3. self-assertive; forward
4. loud-sounding
5. stimulating to the taste
6. sorcerer
7. the act of pouring out

GAME 13

arboretum: a place where trees and plants are grown for scientific and educational purposes.

caryatid: a sculptured draped female figure used as an architectural column.

coloratura: florid ornamentation in vocal music.

colporteur: a peddler of religious books.

demesne: manorial land possessed by the lord and not held by free tenants.

dressage: the execution by a horse of complex maneuvers in response to barely perceptible movements of a rider's hands, legs, and weight.

intaglio: an engraving or incised figure in a hard material(as stone) depressed below the surface of the material.

pithecanthropus: any of several primitive extinct men from Java.

prophylactic: preventing or guarding from disease.

sidereal: measured by the apparent motion of the fixed stars.

xebec: a usu. 3-masted Mediterranean sailing ship with long overhanging bow and stern.

zephyr: a gentle breeze.

zwieback: sweetened bread that is baked and then sliced and toasted until dry and crisp.

GAME 14

ACROSS: 2 - souvenir, 5 - misconduct, 7 - indicate, 11 - adventure, 12 - condition

DOWN: 1 - reduced, 3 - dictionary, 4 - introduction, 6 - inconvenient, 8 - educational, 9 - invent, 10 - verdict

GAME 15

1. A.
2. A.
3. C.
4. B.
5. C.
6. C.
7. B.
8. C.
9. A.
10. B.
11. C.
12. C.
13. C.

14. B.
15. A.
16. C.
17. C.
18. C.
19. C.
20. B.

GAME 16

ACROSS: 1 - dictatorship, 3 - contradictory, 7 - eventful, 9 - aqueduct, 10 - prediction, 11 - prevention
DOWN: 1 - dedicated, 2 - productive, 4 - deduced, 5 - venturesome, 6 - duchess, 8 - conventional

GAME 17

F. bevy
C. covey
E. nide
A. pod
B. skein
G. skulk
D. sounder

GAME 18

E   axilla
D   canthus

F frenum

A glabella

C gular

G lunula

B uvula

GAME 19

SAMSON: a man of extraordinary physical strength.

VANDAL: one who willfully destroys or defaces any work of art or literature.

SOLOMON: a very wise man.

HEGIRA: any flight or exodus regarded as like that of Mohammed.

BARMECIDE: one who proffers some illusory advantage or benefit.

DULCINEA: mistress; a sweetheart.

SOPHIST: an impostor in argument; a captious or fallacious reasoner.

GAME 20

1. c
2. a
3. d
4. b
5. c
6. c

7. d
8. e
9. a
10. b
11. a
12. d
13. d
14. b
15. d